THE STATE AND EDUCATIONAL CHANGE:
Essays in the History of Educational and Pedagogy

THE STATE AND EDUCATIONAL CHANGE:

Essays in the History of Education and Pedagogy

Brian Simon

LAWRENCE & WISHART
LONDON

Lawrence & Wishart Ltd
144a Old South Lambeth Road
London SW8 1XX

First published 1994 by Lawrence & Wishart

Cover design by Jan Brown Designs
Photoset in North Wales by
Derek Doyle & Associates, Mold, Clwyd.
Printed and bound in Great Britain by
Redwood Books, Trowbridge, Wiltshire.

Contents

Introduction

This volume comprises a number of essays, sometimes lectures, written and delivered over the last few years focussing largely on the history of education but also on problems of pedagogy which remains an area of interest and concern. Most of the chapters have been published in one form or another, though several in relatively obscure or professional journals not easy for the general reader to monitor. Three of the chapters (3, 9 and 11) have not been published elsewhere.

The book is divided into three Parts. The single chapter which forms Part One sets out to make a renewed case for the study of the history of education by teachers, students and indeed all those involved in the educational process as a whole. The book, of which it forms the opening chapter, 'Why Should We Teach the History of Education?', comprises contributions from historians of education in several countries. This was the brain child of an old friend, Kadriya Salimova of Moscow, herself an historian of education recently elected as a member of the Russian Academy of Educational Sciences. In spite of all the difficulties in Moscow over the last two or three years, Professor Salimova, who headed a Working Group of the International Standing Conference for the History of Education concerned with this initiative, succeeded in bring this book out. Printed and published (in English) in Moscow in 1993, this is a forerunner of further books being planned internationally under the same auspices. Theoretical studies in education are clearly unpopular among the political authorities in Britain at the moment, though whether historical studies can be so categorised is doubtful. In spite of the cold climate, or rather precisely because of it, I felt challenged, on receiving the invitation to contribute, to attempt to articulate once again some, at least, of the reasons why historical studies remain highly relevant to students, teachers and indeed (perhaps especially) to policy-makers in education.

Part Two contains the bulk of the strictly historical studies in this volume. In the mid-1980s I became involved in an international research project based on the University of Bochum in what was then

West Germany which resulted in the publication of a transnational socio-historical study entitled *The Rise of the Modern Educational System: Structural Change and Social Reproduction, 1870-1920* published by Cambridge University Press in 1987. This was jointly edited by Detlef K. Müller (Germany), Fritz Ringer (United States) and myself. In the first chapter of this book, Detlef Müller elaborates his theory of 'systematisation', utilising it to interpret developments in German secondary education over this period. In the second chapter Fritz Ringer, author of *Education and Society in Modern Europe* (1979) and other works, elaborates his own theory of 'segmentation' and applies it to the case of French secondary education over the same period. My own chapter, on English developments in secondary education at this time, was influenced by both theories as a result of thorough, and lengthy discussions with Müller and Ringer over a considerable period of time. Originally entitled 'Systematisation and segmentation in education: the case of England', it is presented here (slightly abbreviated) under a new title since its major thrust is to emphasise the importance of action by the state in the reconstruction of secondary education during this period – an aspect that has, generally, been overlooked by English historians of education. This essay draws on my own earlier publications in this field, particularly *The Two Nations and the Educational Structure, 1780-1870*, first published as *Studies in the History of Education, 1780-1870* (1960), and *Education and the Labour Movement, 1870-1920* (1965). It does, however, embody an overall analysis which differs in some respects from the theses advanced in these two books. I have to thank Detlef Müller and Fritz Ringer for our many discussions on disputed issues as also my colleague at Leicester University, David Reeder, whose advice and support has been consistently stimulating and helpful. I also owe a debt to David Allsobrook whose unpublished PhD thesis on factors influencing the origins of the Schools Inquiry Commission's report of 1868, casts much light on the social and political factors affecting educational restructuring in England in the period covered by this essay (see his *Schools for the Shires*, Manchester University Press, 1986).

Chapter 3, drafted a few years ago but first published here, is basically a case study on the theme of state intervention in the restructing of English education in the 1860s, focussing on the use made of the technique of Executive Commissioners to soften legislation with the aim of firming up the hierarchic system successfully established at this time. As one educational historian has put it, 'There is no doubt that the late 60s and early 70s marked a decisive stage in the development of education in this country. During it what was possibly the last aristocratic government in English history created a closed system of schools for the governing class' (see p000). That closed system still survives, to the detriment of the wellbeing of the country as a whole. This chapter is concerned to analyse in some detail how this undesirable outcome was assured.

A central aspect of this mid-century reorganisation relates to the hijacking (this seems the *mot juste*) of sometimes very considerable endowments originally bequeathed for the education of local children (usually for 'poor scholars') by the upper middle class, gentry and aristocracy of Victorian times. Chapter 4, an invited address to a conference on 'Schools and Charitable Status – New Ways Ahead?', organised by the Directory of Social Change (January 1992) argues that this situation is no longer either morally or socially acceptable, and that it should be made good through an Act of Restitution, by which these resources are returned to the community. Among the speakers at the conference were Robin Guthrie, Chief Charity Commissioner and David Jewell, Master of Haileybury and recently Chairman of the Headmasters' Conference, who, not surprisingly, presented an opposite view. The papers given at this conference were published in Anne Mountfield, (ed.), *The Charitable Status of Schools: What Needs to be Done?* (Directory of Social Change, 1992).

These three chapters (2, 3 and 4), therefore, form a unity, having a common theme. The next three (in Part Two) are more diverse, though the divided nature of the English educational system, consequent on the successful restructuring of education in the 1860s and 70s, provides the theme of Chapter 5. This reproduces an invited lecture at a conference on 'Quality of Citizenship' held at the University of Utrecht, The Netherlands, in March 1991 and addressed, among others, by Sir Ralf Dahrendorf and Jürgen Habermas. Although the extension of the franchise through successive measures in the nineteenth and twentieth centuries finally accorded the right to vote to all adults, male and female, so assuring full citizenship in this sense, did not the concomitant restructuring process in education, carefully designed to ensure a fractured, divisive system reversing its highest rewards to a small hereditary/financial elite, effectively undermine the possibility of effective participation by all in a full and vibrant citizenship? This is the issue raised in this chapter and left without solution.

Chapter 6, 'The Universities and Social Change', the 1990 Charles Carter lecture at Lancaster University for, is concerned, if perhaps in an oblique manner, with the important theoretical issue of the relation between educational and social change. It is, in a sense, a critique of the more mechanistic reproductionist theories which emanated, a few years ago, both from across the Channel (Pierre Bourdieu, Louis Althusser) and from across the Atlantic at roughly the same time (Bowles and Gintis, Coleman, Jencks). The chapter argues that at specific historical periods, taking Cambridge and Oxford respectively as examples, both universities can claim to have effectively influenced, or even brought about, a radical degree of social change and cannot, therefore, be accused of always reflecting and reinforcing the *status quo*. This chapter may, perhaps, be regarded as part of what seems a life-long campaign supporting the notion that conscious human action *can* be effective and that, in the field of education especially, fatalistic theories leading to political or social quietism must be rejected.

Chapter 7 reverts to the universities and is also historical in its content – if of a time still within the experience and life span of some of us. It attempts a reconstitution and analysis of what was called 'the student movement' of the 1930s. Here was another university-based movement which sought to effect social change largely led, in this case, by students educated within what was then a small group of elite public schools. If this seems to contradict the purposes for which these schools were formed into a 'system' in the late nineteenth century, as analysed in Chapters 2 and 3, this only highlights the thesis of unintended outcomes, dissected in Chapter 6. As President of the National Union of Students in 1939-40, this was a movement of which I had some experience myself.

Part Three contains, perhaps, a more miscellaneous group of essays, two of which (8 and 10) involve historical analyses while two (9 and 11) have a more contemporary significance. Chapter 8 reprints an article I was asked to contribute to the journal *Studies in Higher Education* in 1983 focussing on the different phases which characterised changing concerns in the study of education at universities from the first establishment of University Education Departments in the 1890s – almost precisely a hundred years ago. To this I have added a short postscript covering the last decade. Such studies are now at risk as a result of the Government's clearly stated desire to drive a wedge between the universities (now greatly expanded) and teacher education generally. How successful this effort will be, and how far, if successful, this will affect university studies in education remains to be seen. But one thing is clear – the present is a cold climate for theoretical (and so also historical) studies in education. On the other hand there is no question that the interest in, and motivation for the pursuit of such studies remains powerful.

Some years ago (in 1981) I published an essay entitled 'Why No Pedagogy in England?' which aroused a degree of interest. An invitation to address the Educational Research Network of Northern Ireland in November 1993 seemed to provide an opportunity to update the argument presented there in the light of the new circumstances prevailing after the imposition of a national curriculum and assessment through the Education Act of 1988. I remain grateful to my hosts and audience for their reception of this lecture which, following very closely a tragic event in Northern Ireland, must have seemed far from their primary concerns as citizens. The many teachers and others present, however, may have found the focus on the classroom, teaching and learning, a welcome relief from current pressures. This chapter reprints this lecture under a changed title and in a slightly modified form, to include up to date reference to the government's November 1993 Education Bill covering teacher education and the proposed Teacher Training Agency.

Comprehensive education has been a main interest of mine over the last fifty years and indeed more, having first been involved in discussion of the issue in the late 1930s, when acting as assistant secretary to the Labour Party's newly constituted Education Advisory Committee. This committee sent a firm recommendation in 1939 to Labour's Executive Committee that the multilateral (as the comprehensive idea was then called) school should be adopted as 'immediate practical policy'. Invited to lecture on the topic 'The Politics of Comprehensive Reorganisation' to the History of Education Society in 1992 I took the opportunity to range over that inception of the policy and its subsequent fate. This is reprinted here as Chapter 10.

Finally I have included, as Chapter 11, a lecture I was invited to give to the Education Division of the University of Sheffield in May 1993. I had found the overt, brazen and unashamed politicisation of education by succeeding Secretaries of State, apparently in collusion with the tabloid press, particularly offensive – especially the sustained, and usually unfair attacks on primary schools and their teachers by Kenneth Clarke, then at its height. On the other hand, international comparisons and analysis seems to indicate, historically, that those countries where the state had intervened in education effectively, (Germany, France), were further ahead on many indicators than Britain. I argue, then, that state intervention can be benign and that, in Britain, we need to develop procedures ensuring that this is so. This certainly does not mean handing all power to a Secretary of State, including the power to determine crucial curricula issues according to passing whims as, sadly, we have experienced in this country. To establish democratic and accountable procedures may prove difficult, but experience increasingly indicates its necessity.

It remains to thank my publishers, Lawrence and Wishart, for loyally undertaking yet another book by me, but one which focusses largely on my first love – the history of education. Things are moving with such rapidity in the field of education that a book which is largely concerned with the past may have some value – especially since decisions made long ago, for instance during the 1860s and 70s, still encase our educational structure in what seems almost a concretised strait-jacket. Any 'radical' reform needs to deal with these structures inherited from the past and now largely 'taken for granted', rather than focus on the destabilisation of all that has been positive in our historical experience over the last fifty to a hundred years. We have yet to create a national system of education in Britain. For a reforming government, I suggest, that should be the priority.

Brian Simon
January 1994

Acknowledgements

Thanks are due to Professor Kadriya Salimova and the International Academy for Self-Improvement in Moscow for permission to reprint the paper 'The History of Education: Its Importance for Understanding' from *Why Should we Teach the History of Education?*, edited by Kadriya Salimova and Erwin V. Johanningmeier (1993); to my co-editors Detlef K. Müller and Fritz Ringer, and to Cambridge University Press for permission to reprint 'The State and Educational Change' which was published originally under a different title as chapter 3 of *The Rise of the Modern Educational System: Structural Change and Social Reproduction, 1870-1920* (1987); to the Directory of Social Change for permission to reprint 'Charity and the Public Schools', originally published under a different title in Anne Mountfield, (ed.), *The Charitable Status of Schools: What Needs to be Done?* (1992); to Lancaster University for permission to reprint 'The Universities and Social Change', the 1990 Charles Carter lecture to the University of Utrecht for permission to reprint 'Education and Citizenship in England' from Brita Rang and Jan C. C. Rupp, (eds.), *The Cultural Range of Citizenship: Citizenship and Education in England, Scotland, Germany, the United States and the Netherlands* (1991); to the Editorial Board of *History of Education* for permission to reprint both 'The Student Movement in England and Wales during the 1930s' and 'The Politics of Comprehensive Reorganisation: a Retrospective Analysis', originally published in *History of Education* Vol 16, No 3 (1987) and Vol 21, No 4 (1992) respectively; to the Editorial Board of *Studies in Higher Education* for permission to reprint 'The Study of Education as a University Subject in Britain', published in Vol 8, No 1 (1983), to which a postscript covering the years 1983 to 1993 has been added; to the Educational Research Network of Northern Ireland for permission to reprint 'Some Problems of Pedagogy, Revisited' (published as a pamphlet by ERNNI under the title 'From Plowden to Patten and Beyond'); and to the University of Sheffield Division of Education for permission to include 'The Politicisation of Education: Implications for Teachers', given as a lecture to the Division in May 1993.

Part One

1: The History of Education: Its Importance For Understanding*

Advances and Retreats

Education is about the empowerment of individuals. It is about discovering, and providing the conditions which encourage the fuller development of abilities and skills in every sphere of human activity – artistic, scientific, social and spiritual. But, more generally, education has been strikingly described as the *mode of development of human beings in society*,[1] and, seen in this light, the *process* of education involves all those formative influences, including the family, peer groups, the churches, apprenticeship, neighbourhood and civic relations with which all are involved from the earliest times; relationships growing in complexity, of course, as society itself becomes more complex. Within these sets of inter-relations, organized schooling, which until recently only affected a small proportion of the population, now plays a central role. Together with the family it is the chief means by which new generations are inducted into the future.

It is of crucial importance, therefore, to attempt to penetrate the relations between education and society, between educational and social change. If schools, colleges, universities and teaching and

* From Kadriya Salimova and Erwin V Johanningmeier, *Why Should we teach History of Education?*, The Library of International Academy of Self-Improvement, Moscow, 1993.

3

learning institutions of all kinds are to flourish, and so realize their purpose of empowerment, we need to understand what circumstances hinder or encourage such a situation. This involves historical analysis. Such analysis indicates that there are no simple answers to these questions; that the whole issue is a great deal more complex than might, at first, be realized. There have been times, for instance, in most countries, when everything in the world of education seems to be advancing tumultuously; when the whole field seems animated by a positive spirit; when all seem to be working to the same end; when generous funding is made available, and when it seems that a new breakthrough is about to be made which will result in more widespread, more genuine opportunities for all, even given the continued existence of powerful forces resistant to change.

Most countries have experienced such a movement at least once during this century. If I may take Britain as an example, then I would argue that, in recent years, the 1960s saw precisely such a movement, one having national significance. This period saw, first, a rapid, planned expansion of higher education involving the establishment of many new universities (and the polytechnics), underpinned by the formulation of a twenty year plan of development right across the board – a plan that was fully accepted, supported and resourced, by government. Second, this period saw the start of a locally-based grass roots swing to 'comprehensive' secondary education, again (from 1965) officially supported by government, a movement that sought to bring to an end, in formal terms at least, the divided, fractured, selective system of the past. Nor was this all. This period also saw the first serious recognition, historically, of primary education as a phase of crucial significance; the abandonment of long-established divisive practices (streaming), and the establishment of humane pedagogic means within these schools. Finally, this period also saw a significant decline in the importance (and number) of the private, or 'independent' schools, together with a growing questioning of their legitimacy. This resulted from increased acceptance of the primacy of the publicly provided (state-maintained) system, and so the emergence of a truly national system of education, locally, and democratically, controlled.

There have been other such periods in Britain, but none where the advances appeared so sweeping. In the late nineteenth century (1880-1900), for instance, a system of elementary education having finally been established, the outlines of an 'alternative system' to that inherited from the past (class-based, hierarchic) began to emerge, particularly in the great industrial cities of the Midlands and North. This (unexpected) upthrust embodied new forms of 'higher grade' schools, 'higher tops' in elementary schools, the so-called 'organized science schools', and so on, all emerging from within the elementary system itself. At the same time new institutions were now being created – technical schools and colleges, art colleges, and other such forms, including local universities only now being founded. So there began to emerge, sometimes rapidly, the lineaments of locally controlled, cohesive systems embracing educational facilities from the primary school to the new universities. In this development, local, directly elected School Boards played a crucial role. Women could be elected to these, as were also representatives of the local labour movement. 'Citadels of radicalism' was how the French historian, Elie Halévy, described these Boards and their work, which marked a definite and very positive phase in the evolution of the educational system.[2]

So there have been periods of advance – including, in Britain, other times when hopes were high, for instance, the few years after World War I and World War II. During both these wars progressive acts of parliament were passed embodying consensus views as to desirable advance – in 1918 and again 1944. But study of the history of education, as well as our own experience today, teaches us that, at least under a capitalist social order, educational advance does not take place in a simple linear fashion. Advances at one time are not necessarily followed by yet further positive developments; nor does history indicate any support for the so-called 'Whig' interpretation of economic, social and political affairs generally – that everything gradually, but regularly, consistently and evenly, improves over time.

On the contrary, periods of advance are often followed by a reaction against all that has been achieved; indeed that reaction may be building up just when the advances are most far-reaching and tempestuous. If circumstances (economic, social, political) are then propitious to these 'new' views, the advances previously experienced may be reversed. There can now be a move, more or less rapidly, towards new forms of control, towards overall constraint, the imposition of new divisions, a reversion to once rejected practices within systems, within schools and colleges, accompanied by the ideological transformations necessary once again to legitimize discarded approaches and practices.

In the case of the two examples just given, this was the English experience. The thrust forward of the 1880s and 1890s was deliberately halted by a conservative government with a large majority in Parliament through the passage of the Education Act of 1902. This *abolished* the school boards under whose auspices the advance had taken place, disallowed and, in effect, abolished the higher grade schools, established a selective elitist system of secondary education and removed education from directly elected popular control. In much the same way the thrust forward of the 1960s has been followed by similar measures, embodied in the 1988 Education Act passed again by a large Conservative parliamentary majority. These latter measures were designed to circumvent, and so to weaken, comprehensive secondary education; to marginalize, or thrust aside, the role of local education authorities in controlling local school systems; to develop a competitive, hierarchic structure of schooling through establishment of a market system in education, and to strengthen privatization of the system.

So historical study highlights the variability of educational change: 'the best of times, the worst of times', as Charles Dickens once put it. The cases just described indicate the complexity of the relations between education and society. Even though it is clear that education, and educational institutions, do at certain periods achieve a degree of autonomy (which varies by country and over time), and even though it is this which gives it its power, yet relationships generally in this field are clearly directly subject to wider, more all-embracing economic, social and political developments within society as a whole. Some of these are confined to a single country; others seemingly influence and affect the world as a whole (the 1960s expansion appears to have been a world-wide phenomenon).

Theory and Practice

One of the outstanding characteristics of periods of advance in education appears to be a close link (or bondage) between educational theory and practice, though, paradoxically perhaps, this may also be a characteristic of a period of reaction – and when this is the case it presents particular problems.

For example, the educational theory which was dominant in the 1880s and 1890s in England, when the 'alternative system', just described, was thrusting energetically forward, was directly based on the classic materialist theory of human development, and specifically on its implications for teaching and learning. This tradition, or outlook, was derived from John Locke (particularly his *Essay Concerning Human Understanding*, 1690), but as developed by David Hartley into the form of associationism and then taken further, particularly as regards its educational implications, by Joseph Priestley, James Mill and many others culminating, perhaps, in Alexander Bain's *Education as a Science* published, significantly, in 1879 – just at the moment when the democratic thrust forward, led by the advanced School Boards, was about to take place. Fundamentally it was this theory which underlay the concept of human perfectibility as enunciated by Condorcet, Helvétius and others during the Enlightenment. This led to the view that all were educable – that, as Joseph Priestley argued, the teacher's action must have a necessary effect; and that to achieve positive outcomes the child's surroundings and all the influences to which he or she was subject must be carefully designed and structured to achieve the desired objectives in terms of human development.[3]

It was this theory, if sometimes crudely enunciated, which underlay and indeed legitimized the thrust forward of the late nineteenth century in Britain. It empowered teachers and underpinned their work as educators. In a different, but related form, such theories were also powerful at this time in Germany, particularly Prussia, the Mecca of educationists in the late nineteenth century, where Herbart's ideas, also based on associationist theory, were widely popular among teachers and educators. Indeed Herbartian theories played a very important role also in England and in the western world generally (including the United States) at this time.

It is a striking fact, however, that the hegemony of these ideas and theories was broken in the early years of this century in England and also elsewhere (for instance, the United States), by the thrust of eugenics and biological thinking generally which now accorded the greatest power over individual human development to heredity. We now enter the period of mass elementary education and of what has been described as 'the great 'psychological capture'' of the school.[4] The new theories found their psychological embodiment in the 'science' of psychometry, or mental measurement, and, using these tools, were applied to the schools where they were used for purposes of categorization or selection.

These theories, in contrast to those of Locke, Condorcet and Bain, stressed the limitation of human powers, the narrow function of education which could not enhance that which was 'given' through heredity, and so down-graded the functions of the schools and teachers. Psychometricians (or mental testers) claimed to be able accurately to measure inborn intellectual abilities. Class and other social differences crystallized within hierarchical school systems simply reflected, in this view, the *natural* differences between individuals. All was for the best in the best of all possible worlds.

This ideology, embodied in the theories of mental testing, and developed in Britain by psychologists working within the field of education (for instance, Cyril Burt), precisely reflected, in the sphere of ideas, the economic, social and so the educational stagnation of the inter-war years (1920-1940). Selection, segregation, categorization became the order of the day as everything slowed down. Educational failure on the part of the great majority of the population was explained (and legitimated) as the direct result of inborn limitations – of psychological failure, incapacity of the human mind. So, once again there was a new bonding between theory and practice; but acting, this time, as a powerful force underpinning educational stagnation.

It is significant that this theory, which achieved hegemony over the whole period from the early 1920s, had to be broken – in the sense of critically analysed and rejected – before the advances of the 1960s, described earlier, could be achieved. And indeed, for the historian, it is crucial to understand that there was, in fact, a deliberate, reasoned, conscious rejection of the fatalistic ideas of the inter-war period at the very start of this decade of advance – a clear rejection that was officially accepted and formed the ideological basis for the famous Robbins Report of 1963 which set out the programme of massive, planned expansion in higher education referred to earlier.[5] The rationale for the rejection of the ideas embodied in what may be called the classic standpoint of psychometry was articulated in 'evidence' given to the Robbins Committee by P. E. Vernon and Jean Floud, a leading academic psychologist and sociologist respectively. The former denied the classic theories of psychometry which held that the proportion of any age group capable of profiting from higher education is 'fixed by some immutable distribution of intelligence', while the latter dismissed the concept of a fixed 'pool of ability' as 'scientifically virtually valueless'. The supply of potential students, Floud argued, is a function of 'social change and social policy' and can be altered by changes in that policy. 'What only the few could do yesterday the many can do today.' Nor is there any 'iron law of the national intellect' imposing 'an upper limit on the educational potential of the population'.[6]

This critique heralded a complete and rapid transformation in the leading ideas relating to education. Now the work of psychologists like A. R. Luria and especially L. S. Vygotsky began to penetrate the West, while in the United States, Jerome Bruner and others advocated similar ideas, as also their counterparts in Britain. In the fields of both primary and secondary education the stress was once again laid on the educability of the normal child, but now on a new level of scientific understanding. It was this transformation in ideas and thinking which provided the theoretical underpinning for the thrust forward of the 1960s. Streaming was now rapidly abolished in primary schools, as also the system of selection at eleven into different, but parallel, types of secondary school. The swing to comprehensive secondary education now really got underway, powered by a new understanding of the extent of human educability. One lesson of history, then, concerns the central importance of ideas in the determination of development.

Education and Social Change

A crucial issue to which historical study can and should make a direct contribution, is that of the relation between educational and social change. This affects teachers and all involved in education which, as argued at the start, is essentially about human empowerment. If this is accepted as a major objective, then those working in this field must look to a society in which fuller scope is in fact given to human activity, since it is through activity in a social setting that human powers are realized. And this necessarily involves social change. Further it may be argued, human energy is likely to be more effective the more people believe in their power to effect change – to bend society more nearly to their aspirations. To subscribe to the belief in the mechanistic determination of educational or social change by structural forces outside human control is, on the other hand, a passport to fatalism – and so to inactivity and, finally, despair.

Can education change society? Or, to put it sharply, is the role of education, as it exists in institutionalized form in most advanced countries today, simply to reflect and perpetuate existing social relations? This is a difficult issue about which there has been much controversy. These opposite standpoints are often presented as stark alternatives – as if the answer must be one or the other. The fact that the role of education may differ in different circumstances is not taken into account. This is a possibility which we will return to later.

The view that educational change is crucial to social change has a long history, and has been expressed at different times in different forms. The great humanist educators of the sixteenth century, such as Erasmus and Melanchthon, certainly held this view. For this reason both exerted themselves throughout their lives to effect educational change. The great Moravian educator, Comenius, whose influence was widespread throughout Europe both in his own lifetime and later, fully accepted this standpoint, as did (as already mentioned) the *philosophes* of the Enlightenment (particularly the French, Helvétius and Condorcet). Rousseau in his own way expressed the same view as John Locke, Joseph Priestley and many others in England including, incidentally, Robert Owen who saw education as central to social change, and whose co-operative communities were seen as its vehicle. From Owen this tradition transferred into the modern socialist movement generally in the nineteenth and twentieth centuries.

Recently, however, the idea that education is *the* means by which existing society, with all its divisions, is reproduced has been strongly argued by social scientists, some sociologists and neo-Marxists. This view has been propagated with considerable force by the leading French sociologist, Pierre Bourdieu, who, in his *Reproduction in Education, Society and Culture* (1970) and other writings has advanced a set of tightly argued logically related propositions which lead to the conclusion that the educational structure, together with the pedagogical processes embodied within it, operates to ensure the reproduction of existing social categories, classes or groups. 'The School as Conservative Force', the title of one of Bourdieu's most influential articles, presents his general view very clearly. From this standpoint, education is certainly not seen as a means of bringing about social change.

At just this time (late 1960s, early 1970s) very similar views were expressed elsewhere. In the United States, for instance, Samuel Bowles and Herbert Gintis, in *Schooling in Capitalist America* (1976) argued very ingeniously what has come to be described as the 'correspond-ence theory'; that the educational structure and ethos 'corresponds' to the structure and ethos of the institutions of monopoly capitalism – and, furthermore, that they necessarily must act in this way. The schools, then, are in no position to challenge existing social structures. A few years earlier, in 1966 and 1972 respectively, social scientists in the United States published two highly influential reports, each based on a mass of contemporary data. These, (the Coleman Report and the Jencks Report, as they were known) both reached similar conclusions, popularly encapsulated in the phrase 'schools make no difference' – that is, schooling was shown to have no significant effect either on the pattern of income distribution or on life chances.[7] This again seemed to indicate that education could hardly promote social change.

This was also the view of the leading French Marxist, Louis Althusser, who in 1970, published his well-known essay entitled 'Ideology and Ideological State Apparatuses'. Althusser argued that the education system had taken the place of the Church as the chief means by which the dominant ideology of a class society was perpetuated, and so that society itself. Teachers were inevitably subsumed as agents of ideological domination, and nothing they could do could have any significant effect. Those who took a radical stance, holding that their actions as teachers could have some effect on the nature of society and even bring about social change were, said Althusser, 'a kind of hero', but one could only pity the futility of their efforts.[8]

Oddly enough these fatalistic views, advanced by radicals and neo-Marxists, chimed in with those of conservative educationists who sought to reverse the promise of the transformation of the 1960s. The result was a sort of unholy alliance between ideologists of the left and right, both of which now operated to disempower, or devalue, the claim that educational change could and did affect social change.

Historical study leads to a different conclusion from that of the social scientists just cited. Educational systems, whether centrally controlled (as in France and until recently the Soviet Union) or where primarily locally controlled (as in the United States and in England and Wales) do appear, at least at certain historical periods, to achieve a degree of autonomy from determination by a centralized state or by powerful structural (economic and social) forces. As England is the country I know best, having studied educational developments since 1780 in some detail, I shall take my examples from the experience of this country, though similar examples could certainly be taken from elsewhere.

There is no doubt whatever that the upthrust which took place in the late nineteenth century, already described, was largely, if not entirely, the outcome of a number of disparate local, or regional initiatives and activity. The primary role was certainly played here by the local School

11

tly elected, as we have seen, since 1870, having powers to
tes to finance local developments. Board (elementary)
nly also received a subvention from the state, but the
~~~~~ ~~ ~~~~~ money from the rates gave considerable powers to local
Boards to speed up development and to direct it in the manner these
thought fit. Hence the upsurge of new, higher level types of schools
and colleges which boded still further advances in the future. The
School Boards' electoral system comprised an advanced form of
proportional representation, unlike parliamentary representation in
Britain; this ensured that all the major political and religious groupings
could be represented on the School Boards, so that positive policies at
this level achieved a genuine consensus.

It was these conditions which, at that time, certainly allowed a
degree of autonomy to the local 'alternative' systems which emerged
with some rapidity in the 1880s and especially the 1890s. Indeed so far
was this perceived to be the case that, very early in the twentieth
century, a conservative government determined to put an end to this
threat (as it was perceived). The steps taken by this government have
already been outlined. The 1902 Education Act, and related measures,
were clearly designed to halt this upthrust from below, and to bring
developments in secondary and higher education more directly under
central control. These measures involved the actual abolition of the
School Boards as we have seen. They also involved clear central control
and limitation of secondary education (in the new county grammar
schools), as well as a very precise central control over the curriculum in
these schools. All this, I would argue, indicates that education had very
definitely achieved a certain autonomy and was therefore in a position
to effect social change. It was this autonomy which was directly
threatened by the series of parliamentary and administrative measures
which focused around the 1902 Education Act.

A strikingly similar pattern of events has taken place more recently
in England, relating to the upthrust of the 1960s.[9] Here again there can
be no question that the main educational developments at this period
were the direct outcome of widespread local, popular activity
determined to put an end to the fractured, diversive system of the past
and to substitute something more generous, more equitable, more
suited to the growing aspirations of the mass of the parents. This
locally based movement was the force that lay behind the struggle for
the single, comprehensive secondary school as well as the movement to
abolish early and rigid streaming in primary schools. Very many

12

examples could be given of the widespread activities which ensured that local education authorities all over the country voted democratically to make the transition to comprehensive education in spite of consistent, and long established, opposition to this policy by both Conservative *and* Labour governments in the whole period 1945-1963. It was the strength of local movements of this kind which finally forced governments of both persuasions to modify their policies so that the Labour government elected in 1964 finally decided fully to encourage this transition.

But, precisely as in the late nineteenth century, these advances provoked a backlash. A series of measures brought in, again by Conservative governments in the 1980s, culminating in the 1988 Education Act were designed to circumscribe, or even destroy, the degree of autonomy which education had once again won back, following the constraining measures at the start of the century. The 1988 Act, as is well known, aims once again to reduce the power of local authorities over their 'systems'. Schools are encouraged to 'opt out' from local authority control; new types of school directly financed by the central state are being established (for instance, city technology colleges); financial control of schools is being devolved from local authorities; a centrally determined curriculum involving mass testing of all pupils covering the ages five to sixteen is being imposed on all maintained schools. So the relative autonomy achieved by local authorities by the 1960s is being destroyed, while that achieved also by the teachers, in terms of influence over the curriculum, is also being swept away. The 1988 Act accorded the Secretary of State for Education and Science some three hundred new powers. To obviate the experience of the 1960s, it seems, direct central state control over all important aspects of education at all levels is being imposed – or such, at least, is the intention. It is evident that the more the educational system is successfully subjected to a strict central control, the less scope there is to affect social change.

What conclusion can we reach? It seems clear that the English experience, at least, indicates that there have been periods of more or less rapid educational advance, based on local, popular movements and implying a critique of the existing social order together with its institutional support network – that is, carrying with it the implication of perhaps even radical social change. Such periods have been followed by periods of reaction characterized by measures preventing further developments, reducing the scope for local, popular control and imposing previously unacceptable levels of direct central control – the objective clearly being to obstruct further change, either educational or social. Where measures of this kind achieve primacy the link between educational and social change is broken; education resumes its conservative function of ensuring reproduction of existing social relations in Bourdieu's sense. There is, then, no simple answer to the question as to whether education can effect social change. The relation between education and society varies over time, and in respect to different circumstances. Nor is there anything fixed or determined about this relationship.

There is, then, considerable scope for human action in determining development – and this is the important point to bear in mind.

Education as a Site of Struggle

Any interpretation of educational change must take account of the fact that different social classes and groupings develop and articulate policies, and indeed a general outlook, reflecting their own needs and aspirations. Advanced industrial societies are, of course, riven by contradictions and divisions between opposing social forces. Such divisions and the conflicts to which they give rise, are necessarily reflected in the world of education – sometimes directly. The result is that education becomes, and is best seen as, a site of struggle between what are often opposing, or at least antagonist social forces. Such conflicts can become acute, as the historical record shows very clearly.

This interpretation was borne in on me when I first tried to make sense of developments in England during the late eighteenth and nineteenth centuries. Finally the model that seemed to 'fit' developments most clearly and logically was the three class model delineated in the writings and analysis of Karl Marx who, of course, derived much of his own material from the data of English industrialization. From the mid-late eighteenth century there took place an energetic development of capitalism which brought into being, and strengthened, the industrial and commercial middle class as a specific sector, one which rapidly became conscious of itself as a class in the early nineteenth century and which now articulated a specific educational policy both for its own members and for the newly developing working class.

With the growth of factory production at this time there also came into being a working class, also now becoming conscious of itself as a

14

class, a process brilliantly analysed by Edward Th
study, *The Making of the English Working Cla*
conditions of early capitalism forced this class t
their circumstances in the struggle for a better li
and power in the early nineteenth century the n
also articulated an educational policy, sou_
themselves, and established a very wide network of educational
activities which reached a climax in the Chartist period (1838-1848),
and again later towards the end of the century.

At the start of the nineteenth century these two classes naturally
confronted the hegemony of the aristocracy and gentry – the land-
owners – who traditionally had ruled the country through the
eighteenth century and earlier. At the start of the century there
developed an alliance between capitalists and workers aiming to force
concessions from the ruling forces. Following their relative success in
the passage of the Reform Act of 1832, however, this alliance was
disrupted and, with the rapid development of industry through the
century, and so of the size and strength of the working class, the
middle class gradually formed an alliance and even fused with the
gentry and aristocracy. The outcome was the establishment, by the end
of the century, of a hierarchical education system catering separately
for each social level, with the so-called 'public' schools (Eton,
Winchester) at the top and the elementary schools for the working
class at the bottom. So the scene was set for further struggles.

Using this model as a basis, it was possible to analyse the very
complex educational developments in England in the nineteenth
century in a way that seemed enlightening and that comprehended
contemporary movements both in the institutional field and in that of
ideas (relating to educational aims and purposes). Though published
now over thirty years ago,[10] no alternative interpretation has been
advanced, while the theses put forward have in fact been generally
accepted both by educational and social historians. Later volumes in
this (historical) series, one covering the period 1870-1920, another the
inter-war period 1920-1940 and a fourth, recently published, the war
and post-war periods 1940-1990 continue this analysis, although the
three class model adopted for the first volume ceases to be appropriate
certainly from the early twentieth century.[11] But that education
continues to act as a site of struggle between opposing social forces
certainly remains the case through the twentieth century and up to
today. Indeed, at the moment of writing, it is more evident than ever.

thing that emerges very clearly is the insistent pressure, from below, to open up the educational system and to ensure fuller access by disadvantaged classes and groups. This pressure meets continuous resistance from those social forces that wish to retain and strengthen existing hierarchical structures in order to ensure that education fulfils its favoured role of facilitating the reproduction of a class divided society. It is the continuous nature of this struggle that ensures that educational development never proceeds in a simple linear form, with everything improving all the time (as education historians of the past often presented the matter). On the contrary, educational development is the outcome of hard, and often very sharp struggles. Advances are recorded, or achieved, when conditions are favourable; retreats at other times.

The nature, procedures and structures of educational systems are clearly of profound significance in terms of human development. It is natural that there should be hard fought battles on these issues. This is why education can best be seen as a site of struggle.

The Importance of Historical Study

In a seminal little book, published fifty years ago in 1940, Sir Fred Clarke, then Director of the Institute of Education, University of London, argued for a new approach to the history of education.[12] This should interpret thought and practice in the past in the light of conflicting social interests and their political expression. It is from this conflict of interests, as Clarke consistently emphasized, that educational change has emerged – in a form tempered by the political settlement arrived at, as well as compromises of thought and practice.

This is, in fact, the direction that historical studies have taken over the past decades in the United Kingdom, the USA and throughout Europe generally. In an essay on this topic written twenty five years ago, I argued that students, teachers – indeed all those concerned with the educational enterprise – would find the historical approach highly relevant to their work in schools and colleges of all types. By setting educational developments in their historical perspective, such study and knowledge 'opens the teachers' eyes to the real nature of their work'. It is the most difficult thing in the world, the essay continued, 'to view *objectively* a system in which one is immediately involved'. Historical study can be a powerful means to this end. 'It enables the student to understand that educational "principles" contain historical components, some of which may no longer be relevant – or, in the light of advancing knowledge, viable – and which are, therefore, open to reconsideration.' The same applies to institutions which have often changed in the past and will certainly be changed in the future. 'There is, perhaps, no more liberating influence than the knowledge that things have not always been as they are and need not remain so.'[13]

Fred Clarke also laid great stress, and correctly in my view, on the need for 'critical awareness' in teachers, and on the place of historical study in promoting this outlook. In his book he argued that to live unquestioningly in the immediate present is to run the danger of developing a conditioned response to current practice: a set of attitudes unconsciously determined rather than consciously formed. The individual teacher, after completing his or her training, enters a school which is part of an immense, ongoing system, governed by rules and procedures which have built up over time and over which he or she has no apparent control. By their very nature, educational institutions tend to be conservative – resistant to changes made necessary by economic and social developments quite outside the schools. Unless the teachers develop a critical awareness as to their role and function, such systems may become dominated by routinism and so lose touch with the wider society in which they exist and which they serve. Historical understanding can alert teachers to this danger, and, together with the critical awareness that Fred Clarke stressed, can provide the motivation for that innovation and change which is essential if education is to make the contribution to social advance which is, in essence, its *raison d'être*. Such an approach not only lends a new interest and excitement to the job of teaching, it should also ensure that the crucial contribution the teaching profession can make to more human social objectives is widely recognized and appreciated by society as a whole.

For all these reasons, I suggest, the historical study of education is important. Such study should surely form part of the teacher's induction as a student, and should be represented in initial training courses in colleges and universities. But the student, preparing to teach, inevitably focuses his or her mind and energies primarily on acquiring the classroom skills needed to survive in schools and to operate as an effective teacher. It is only when he or she has acquired these basic skills that minds and energies are freed for more intensive study of the social determinants of education. It is at this stage, through in-service courses and similar approaches, that the serious and committed teacher can most fruitfully give time and energy to historical study and reading. At this stage such study is most rewarding; indeed it is essential as the means of completing the formation of a truly professional teacher.

I have attempted, in this essay, to set out some of the main conclusions I have reached as a result of the detailed study involved in the production of four volumes covering the history of education in England from 1780 to the present day (1990). The focus is broadly on the relations between educational and social change since this is the crucial issue that confronts the historian. The complexities of this relationship are, of course, many and varied, and far greater than indicated here. These cannot be dealt with in a short essay. I have, therefore, attempted to focus only on essentials. I hope that students and teachers, in particular, may find this contribution helpful.

Notes

[1] Joan Simon, «The History of Education in *Past and Present*», *Oxford Review of Education*, 3, 1 (1977).

[2] Elie Halévy, *Imperialism and the Rise of Labour*, 1961 ed.

[3] For Priestley's views and those of the English Enlightenment, see Brian Simon, *Studies in the History of Education, 1780-1870*, London, 1960, Chapter 1.

[4] David McCallum, *The Social Production of Merit: Education, Psychology and Politics in Australia 1900-1950*, London, 1990.

[5] Higher Education, Report of the Committee on Higher Education (the Robbins Report), Cmnd 2165, 1963.

[6] For Vernon and Floud's evidence to the Robbins Committee, see *Higher Education, Report*, Part II, *Evidence*.

[7] James Coleman et al., *Equality of Education Opportunity*, Washington, 1966; Christopher Jencks et al., *Inequality: A Reassessment of the Effect of Family and Schooling in America*, New York, 1972. My analysis of the work of Bowles and Gintis, Bourdieu (in the previous paragraph) and Althusser (in the next) draws on my essay 'Can Education Change Society?', in Brian Simon, *Does Education Matter?* London, 1985.

[8] Louis Althusser, «Ideology and Ideological State Apparatuses», in *Lenin and Philosophy and Other Essays*, London, 1970, pp121-173.

[9] The term «England» is used here rather than Britain, since Scottish developments in this period differ strikingly from English.

[10] As *Studies in the History of Education, 1780-1870*, London, 1960. This volume was later retitled as *The Two Nations and the Educational Structure, 1780-1870*, London, 1974.

11 *Education and the Labour Movement, 1870-1920*, London, 1965; *The Politics of Educational Reform, 1920-1940*, London, 1974; *Education and the Social Order, 1940-1990*, London, 1991.

12 Fred Clarke, *Education and Social Change*, London, 1940.

13 Brian Simon, 'The History of Education', in: J W Tibble, ed., *The Study of Education*, London, 1966.

Part Two

Part Two

2: The State and Educational Change, 1850-1870*

In considering educational change in England in the mid to late nineteenth century it may be as well, first, to define what features appear as specific to England at this period, compared with France and Germany. There are two aspects which should be stressed: the first concerns chronology, or the sequence of events; the second, the means by which the transformation was brought about.

The State and Educational Change, 1850-70

First, as I have argued in detail elsewhere, the crucial 'moment of change' in England was the period 1850 to 1870.[1] It was during these twenty years that a series of Royal Commissions were appointed, with the brief of examining and making recommendations for the reform of all levels of education from the elementary schools to the ancient universities, and including, as a crucial aspect, the provision of schooling for the various strata of the middle and professional classes, gentry and aristocracy. Each of these Commission reports was succeeded by the passage of an Act of Parliament which laid down the statutory basis for reform. The patterning and restructuring that resulted (which, of course, was inevitably based to some extent on contemporary developments within the institutions concerned) began to be implemented from the 1860s on, but it was in the last decades of

* From Detlef K. Müller, Fritz Ringer and Brian Simon (eds.), *The Rise of the Modern Educational System, Structural Change and Social Reproduction*, Cambridge University Press and La Maison des Sciences de L'Homme, 1987, Chapter 3 (re-titled).

the century that this restructuring became firmly grounded in institutional change. The full consequences, and implications, of the measures determined between 1850 and 1870 were by no means immediately realised, but took several years fully to work themselves out.

Second, as also argued elsewhere, this restructuring was brought about by the direct intervention of the state.[2] The technique used – that of the appointment of a Royal Commission, normally with powers to require submission of 'evidence', subsequent publication of the Commission's report and evidence (often in many volumes), followed by public discussion and Parliamentary debate leading to the passage of a Parliamentary Act – was one which was widely used by reforming Parliaments in the nineteenth century (for instance, in relation to the Poor Laws, Municipal Reform and so on). This clear involvement by the state has not, traditionally, been accorded its full significance by historians of education, who have tended to interpret state intervention in England only in terms of the development of elementary education – from the point when the state was directly involved in making financial grants to such schools (from 1833) and the subsequent foundation of an Education Department to administer such grants. The central role played by the state in the restructuring of secondary and higher education in mid-century has tended to be ignored while attention was focused, in the latter half of the century, on the elementary Education Act of 1870 and subsequent developments in this field.[3]

While no direct financial support was provided by the state either for secondary or for university education in the mid-nineteenth century, the transformation brought about through state intervention (and subsequent legislation) was directly concerned with the redistribution (and the use) of actually existing financial resources, which were then seen, in a sense, as a public trust. These were the endowments, sometimes substantial, which assisted in the financing of most grammar and 'public' schools, as well as the universities of Oxford and Cambridge. It is this point that is overlooked. The restructuring that took place involved not only the transformation of existing institutions and the emergence (to some extent) of new institutions (for instance, girls' grammar schools),[4] but also the relations between the different levels or 'subsystems' that were developed with each other and with the state. In all this the role of the state, as exemplified by the new statutory requirements and the actions of Commissioners with executive powers appointed to carry these through, was of primary significance.[5]

These issues will be considered in more detail later. In the meantime two points may be made in a comparative study of this kind. First, in England,[6] conflicts between different social groupings leading to a basic restructuring of education, which were fought out with considerable energy during the first half of the century, led to decisive action some twenty to thirty years earlier than was the case in France and Germany. This, it seems probable, was the outcome of the earlier impact of industrialisation and urbanisation in England compared with the Continental countries. In particular, the continuous critique, by representatives of the new industrial and commercial middle class (represented in the early years of the century by the utilitarians, or philosophic radicals, led by Bentham and Mill) as well as by other sections of the population (for instance, advanced groupings of the emerging working class, now becoming conscious of itself as a class), reached a point of what might be called crisis by the early 1850s. At this point the industrial middle class, which had been gaining economic power and wealth with great rapidity, now also gained a measure of political power through increased representation in Parliament, partly as a result of the Reform Act of 1832 – an increased power epitomised in their victory over the repeal of the Corn Laws in 1846. At the same time, the traditional educational institutions – Oxford and Cambridge and the leading 'public' and grammar schools – were being perceived as increasingly dysfunctional and were themselves undergoing a crisis of survival (particularly the 'great' schools such as Winchester, Westminster and Charterhouse). It was this concatenation of circumstances, embodying different (and even opposite) perspectives on the part of widely differing social groups or classes, that created a climate where change, reform and even transformation now came on the agenda, the need for it being widely recognised.

It is along these lines, it may be suggested, that an explanation can be found as to why it was that decisive, even ruthless measures were determined on in the period 1850 to 1870. To put the matter simply (and, no doubt, crudely), there was, on the one hand, a growing pressure for reform from those sections of society (middle and working classes) that wanted change and modernisation and who were demanding access to a set of transformed educational institutions, and, on the other, a growing realisation on the part of the dominant sections of the social hierarchy (gentry and aristocracy) of the urgent need for reform if the traditional institutions of the country were to preserve their hegemony and not be supplanted by new institutions representing the interests and aspirations of new social classes – now perceived as representing a serious threat to the established order.

The second point, to which I have already referred, concerns the means by which this restructuring was brought about. In France, for historical reasons, the state certainly played a major role in the control and shaping of the educational structure, at least since Napoleonic times. In Germany, the Prussian state had also been involved at all levels, at least from the early years of the century, and, as Prussia expanded after 1866 through the assimilation of new principalities such as Hanover, a degree of centralised planning was directed towards ensuring development on uniform lines (in both the *Gymnasien* and universities) in the new, expanded Prussia and, after 1870, in the new unified Germany. England is generally regarded as exceptional in that it has been held that the state was not directly involved in controlling or shaping the system. While it is certainly the case that direct control over individual institutions was never exercised, nevertheless in the restructuring of the system as a whole, as has been argued, a crucial role was in fact played by the state. Indeed, without intervention on the scale experienced, such a finely defined restructuring as was achieved could hardly have taken place. The interesting point is that this process involved features of systematisation and segmentation very similar to that brought about in France and Germany a generation later.

There is one further, and perhaps modifying, feature that might be stressed at the start. This is the important role that market forces were able to play in England before, during and after the overall restructuring that took place. Before 1850-60 some grammar schools, for instance, were already tapping what might be called the national market, so that a process of differentiation was, in a sense, endemic in the situation. Again, in the latter decades of the century, a clear tension developed between market forces and government-inspired blueprints so far as the endowed schools were concerned; such tensions clearly affected outcomes.

Here also, then, was an important difference between the situation in England and that in France and Germany, where market forces seem less influential. There was, in England, nothing equivalent to the system of state certification widely developed in Germany. Qualification for different levels of employment depended more directly on the status conferred by schooling – a situation which again gave scope to market forces in determining the process of school differentiation and therefore the nature of the hierarchical system that resulted.

Social Class and Educational Change

Any attempt to 'make sense' of the overall transformation of education in England at this time – from a relatively inchoate structure at the beginning of the century to a system comprising a finely differentiated or segmented set of interrelated 'subsystems' at the close – must involve definition of the main social forces bringing it about. As a preliminary generalisation, study of the period and of succeeding events seems to indicate that the factors involved (specifically in the differentiation process) were primarily of a social and political character rather than directly economic.

Changes in the economy based on scientific and technological advance certainly underlay social developments in the nineteenth century. The growth of industry, commerce and banking led not only to the formation of new social classes – in particular of an industrial and commercial middle class and, with the growth of factory production, of the working class or proletariat – but also to an increasing complexity of occupational structure, in particular among what may be called the middle strata – professional and other white-collar occupations. Indeed, Geoffrey Holmes has recently analysed, in a fascinating study, the extraordinary rise of the professions in the early eighteenth century, a process which continued with considerable force through the eighteenth and early nineteenth centuries.[7]

In addition, the first half of the century, following the traumatic experience of the French Revolution, which had its repercussions in England as well as elsewhere, was a period of sharp social conflict and instability, when even the new power of capital itself was under attack. In this sense, powerful economic and political factors certainly underlay the educational changes of the mid-century. These, however, it appears, were mediated through changes in the occupational structure which directly led to new demands on, or requirements of, an educational system that reflected the needs of an earlier dispensation. The fact that institutional change was already taking place under the influence of market forces early in the century has already been mentioned. This, however, partly as a result of legal conditions as then

27

interpreted, was inadequate to meet the force of criticism and pressure, which had mounted considerably by mid-century.[8]

As restructuring (of individual institutions as well as sets of institutions) became a political necessity, conflict about its nature necessarily surfaced. It seems that the dominant social forces of the time were now able to use the situation so created to determine the direction and character of this restructuring. Without these forces necessarily having clear overall intentions, the fact is that the *outcome* of this overall restructuring was the establishment of a system which reflected – and provided for – different levels in the hierarchy of social strata then existing. As the Schools Inquiry Commission was to put it, 'education has become more varied and complex ... the different classes of society, the different occupations of life, require different teaching'.[9] It could be said that the function of education emerging from the measures adopted in mid-century was not so much that of ensuring the *reproduction* of society with a divided social structure as the actual reinforcement and more precise refinement of an hierarchical society in which each stratum knew, was educated for, and accepted, its place.

Discussing mid-Victorian education, the historian Geoffrey Best, for instance, characterises the changes made as not only creating a system which reflected class differences, but as being deliberately patterned to perpetuate them. 'Educational systems', he writes, 'can hardly help mirroring the ideas about social relationships of the societies that produce them.' Education became a 'trump card' in the great class competition. The result was that the schools of Britain 'not only mirrored the hierarchical social structure ... but were made more and more to magnify its structuring in detail'.[10] So, in Best's view, education reinforced and exacerbated class differences. This view is generally held among historians. Thus Harold Perkin characterises developments in the 1860s as intended 'to put education in a straitjacket of social class'.[11]

Such analyses, in terms of social class, clearly owe much to Marx's approach. However, the Marxist theory concerning the relation between changes in the economic base (or 'forces of production') and the 'superstructure' (law, ideology, institutions, for instance), while having a clear significance in terms of overall revolutionary change as, for instance, from one economic-social formation to another (e.g. feudalism to capitalism), cannot be taken to imply a direct, linear (or mechanistic) relationship between 'base' and 'superstructure' within a given economic-social formation, as is argued by some Marxists and even neo-Marxists (for instance, Bowles and Gintis, whose 'correspondence theory' reflects such an approach).[12] Such a 'model' runs the danger of vulgarising Marxism.

The issue, it seems, is a great deal more complex than is recognised within such formulations. Education as a system comprising what are often powerful and interrelated institutions has, it is now generally accepted, a certain 'autonomy' (or a 'relative autonomy'). In the Marxist sense this implies that educational institutions and ideologies are not *directly* affected by changes in the economic structure (in Bourdieu's sense it seems to mean that education has a certain *apparent* independence from the state and dominant social forces, so that it ensures more effectively its function of securing social reproduction).[13] Specific developments in education, as in mid-nineteenth-century England, appear above all, as mentioned earlier, to be subject both to market forces and to political pressures, influences and measures. These latter, which appear dominant in any organised action by the 'state', primarily reflect the interests of dominant social classes (or class alliances). It is in the interpretation of the formation of such classes (and strata), and of the changing relationship between social classes, their conflicts and alliances insofar as these affect, or are embodied in, their educational actions, that the Marxist approach can be helpful – if only in giving an overall orientation to such interpretations.

In England, for instance, modernisation of the educational system dates from the Reformation.[14] It was at this period – from the early mid-sixteenth to the mid-seventeenth century – that 'grammar schools' were established in most market towns, with separate school buildings being erected and teaching being developed as a profession, and that a systematic approach to the structuring of the content of education (the curriculum) took root. Two or three hundred years later, in the mid-nineteenth century, as a result of industrialisation and the social changes that resulted, that system stood in urgent need of reform if it was to meet both the new pressures and demands arising from occupational change and the perceived requirements of social strategy in terms of maintaining, or reinforcing, social stability. It is something of a paradox that, by the end of the century, what actually transpired was not so much a system reflecting the needs of the economy (for instance, giving primacy to science and technology and being open-ended and supportive of individualised endeavour, as perhaps in the United States), as the creation of a set of more or less closed subsystems of institutionalised education at different levels, which were only articulated together to a limited extent and, as Best and Perkin describe it, had the primary function of reinforcing class divisions. It is these developments that require explanation.

Education and the Industrial Bourgeoisie

It is striking fact that, in spite of the rapidity and force of industrialisation in England, and so of scientific and technological change, no serious attempt was made in the middle of the century to create new forms of education specifically related to this energetic upthrust; or, if such attempts were made, their success was marginal.

It is worth remembering that in the closing decades of the eighteenth century Literary and Philosophical Societies, which united industrialists, scientists and professional men (particularly medical men), did in fact give priority to, and were successful in creating, just such institutions – the Manchester College of Art and Sciences, for instance, as well as the Manchester Academy in the dissenting, but now Unitarian tradition.[15] These provincial Societies, the most famous of which was, of course, the Lunar Society grouped around Boulton and Watt at Soho in Birmingham, were directly concerned with scientific investigation and advance, and with its practical application in the new technologies of the day (particularly the chemical industry related to cotton manufacture). Members of these groupings were profoundly interested in education, if for their own children and groupings in particular, and advanced new theories which embodied a philosophically materialist outlook and an all-round humanist-scientific perspective.[16]

These institutions, however, did not survive in their original form far into the nineteenth century. The new spokesmen of the industrial middle class – the utilitarians – narrowed the perspectives of their predecessors, although again emphasising the need for modern knowledge and a total reformation of the curriculum. Such a programme is best epitomised in Bentham's *Chrestomathia*, his plan for a new school on new lines which it was hoped could be erected in Leicester Square (in London).[17] This deliberately rejected the procedures and ethos of the traditional institutions of the country by embodying a specifically utilitarian approach to education, with the curriculum determined by the two principles of utility and facility (the promotion of ease of understanding through the logical arrangement of the sequence of studies).

It was at this period – in the 1820s and early 1830s – that what might be called a specifically *bourgeois* (or middle-class) thrust in education began to express itself forcibly. The establishment first of University College (1828) and later of the University of London (1836) again reflected the aspirations and objectives of social groupings excluded, for religious, financial or other reasons, from the ancient universities. University College certainly embodied new conceptions as to the role, character and function of a university and was seen as a clear challenge by Oxford and Cambridge, who fought its establishment extremely bitterly.

There was, then, a definite thrust from the new social forces at this time. This period also saw the founding of a whole set of interconnected institutions in the provincial cities, particularly those of the Midlands and the North, which were developed throughout the middle years of the century. These cities were the home of a scientific culture (epitomised by the important part played by the Literary and Philosophical Societies), of an independent liberal press (for instance, the *Manchester Guardian* and the Leeds *Mercury*) and of a series of cultural institutions (Athenaeums, for example), while the whole culture was linked together through the espousal, often by the leading industrialists, merchants and professional men, of Non-conformism, and especially of Unitarianism. These institutions played a dominant and crucial role in many provincial cities in mid-century, and of course earlier (especially after 1835, with the passage of the Municipal Reform Act).[18]

There was, then, a clear challenge to the hegemony of the culture of the gentry and aristocracy as embodied in traditional educational institutions. However, it was not this trend and these interests which carried all before them in the process of restructuring between 1850 and 1870, and later. In fact, developments took an opposite direction. Study of the classics – the traditional subject matter of the curriculum – was revitalised in the latter half of the century as the curriculum considered appropriate to the Victorian upper middle class. The ethos, mores and indeed the institutions of traditional education became the models increasingly accepted by the middle class and the new social forces now bidding for hegemony. The culture of the gentry and aristocracy was in fact accepted by leading sections of the bourgeoisie – perhaps predominantly by that section defined recently by Rubinstein as comprising those involved in commerce and finance (based in

London), rather than industry (based in the North).[19] It seems that this new class, now achieving positions of power, took over the existing symbols of dominance and excellence, which still retained their significance. However this may be, there is no doubt that the challenge from the new social forces was now muted. The educational objectives of the new middle class now became ambivalent.

Even if it seems strange and contradictory, it is worth recalling that Gladstone himself, leader of the great reforming Liberal Party from the 1860s on, was himself the son of a Liverpool merchant of Scottish (and trade) descent, had himself been schooled at Eton, was himself a distinguished classical scholar and, in a well-known letter to the Royal Commission on the Public Schools (the Clarendon Commission), stated his firm conviction that only a classical education was, or could be, appropriate to that small section of the population destined to attend the leading 'public' schools and then to assume responsibility for governing the country. Indeed, he went so far as to suggest that Greek civilisation had been providentially brought into being precisely to provide a suitable subject matter for the education of the English gentleman![20]

Engels' comments on the bourgeoisie at this time are very relevant to this analysis. 'In England', he wrote (in 1892),

> the bourgeoisie never held undivided sway. Even the victory of 1832 left the landed aristocracy in almost exclusive possession of all the leading government offices. The meekness with which the wealthy middle class submitted to this remained inconceivable to me until the great Liberal manufacturer, Mr W E Forster, in a public speech implored the young men of Bradford to learn French, as a means to get on in the world, and quoted from his own experience how sheepish he looked when, as a Cabinet Minister, he had to move in a society where French was at least as necessary as English.

The fact was, Engels goes on,

> The English middle class of that time were, as a rule, quite uneducated upstarts, and could not help leaving to the aristocracy those superior government places where other qualifications were required than mere

insular narrowness and insular conceit, seasoned by business sharpness
... Thus, even after the repeal of the Corn Laws, it appeared as a matter
of course that the men who carried the day, the Cobdens, Brights,
Forsters, etc., should remain excluded from a share in the official
government of the country, until 20 years afterwards a new Reform Act
opened to them the door of the Cabinet.[21]

Even then, their representation remained small. In 1869 John Bright
entered the Cabinet. In 1880, Joseph Chamberlain. But by now a new
phase had opened.

In the period of restructuring, the traditional classical education was
legitimated anew in the reformed institutions for the middle and upper
classes, as we shall see. Science, although strongly pressed (by
scientists), for instance in evidence to the Clarendon Commission, was
regarded as of inferior value and relegated to subsidiary streams or
institutions – an example of segmentation as interpreted by Ringer.
Technology was not, at this time, even considered as a possible
appropriate subject matter for these classes.

Nor did science and its application in technology gain more than a
slippery foothold at other levels until the 1880s and 1890s, when there
were a number of developments of some significance, particularly
concerning the development of the new universities and colleges in the
great provincial cities (Manchester, Birmingham, Leeds, Sheffield,
Newcastle, Bristol) as well as London. At this point there were also
significant developments at lower levels, including the beginning of the
upthrust of the higher grade (elementary) schools and the system of
'organised science schools', financed through the Department of
Science and Art, which now came into being, again largely in the great
provincial cities of the Midlands and the North. Nevertheless it
remains true that in England industrial development in mid to late
century still owed little to institutionalised education.[22] Towards the
close of the century another factor began to influence the situation –
the development of imperialism. The massive export of capital that this
entailed – the seeking of a higher rate of profit by investment abroad
than could be obtained in England – militated against the
modernisation of the technical and industrial base, for this was held
not to be necessary.[23] This factor clearly operated against ensuring
high levels of scientific and technological education, even if, as in the
mid-1880s, a powerful pressure group like the National Association
for the Promotion of Technical Education now began to press for

change and to compare English developments in the area adversely to what they perceived to be happening in Germany, Switzerland and other European countries by this time – a point of view also strongly pressed by the Royal Commission on Technical Education, which reported in 1884.

What, then, was the basis of the restructuring and systematisation of education in nineteenth-century England? As indicated earlier, although the industrial bourgeoisie in the great provincial cities did develop their own scientific culture and specific religious outlook (Non-conformism), this hardly found expression in a coherent educational policy or ideology in the crucial mid-century years;[24] nor did they then articulate any overall proposals for action for educational change for the middle and upper strata, either locally or nationally. Those grouped around the Anti-Corn Law League of the 1840s focused their thrust in the Lancashire-led campaign for the provision of popular education for the working classes, founding the Lancashire (later, the National) Public Schools Association and campaigning energetically in the 1850s for rate-supported, locally and democratically controlled, secular (or non-sectarian) systems of elementary education.[25]

As far as other classes were concerned, the initial thrust both of the Unitarians in the late eighteenth century and of the utilitarians in the 1820s and 1830s was forgotten, or at least not developed further into a specific programme of change – though the influence of Bentham's mid-century followers such as Chadwick, Nassau Senior and even Henry Brougham, who was still active, should not be under-estimated. Nevertheless, as David Allsobrook has shown in a recent detailed study,[26] the main force or thrust for change locally, regionally and ultimately nationally now came from the traditionally dominant classes – the landed gentry and aristocracy, assisted by the specific expertise of representatives of the professional groupings linked traditionally with these classes. Among these, Frederick Temple, headmaster of Rugby and later Archbishop of Canterbury, played a leading part, drafting two of the crucial chapters of the Schools Inquiry Commission Report, while James Bryce and T. H. Green, both Assistant Commissioners, particularly the latter, influenced the final recommendations concerning grading and restructuring.[27]

These groupings were concerned to restructure, and to some extent to modernise, local and, later, national systems of schools – not so much for themselves, but more particularly for the various levels of the

middle class (farmers, the professions and the minor g
artisans). They now formed 'County committees', ma
in agricultural education and sought to link the re
'systems' with Oxford University by establishing
appropriate to this initiative.[28] Among them the liberal a͜   ͜were
also becoming closely concerned about the possible alienation of
professional and business elements in the middle class from the largely
Anglican-dominated universities and endowed grammar schools, and
were themselves considering the need to restructure education in the
cities as well as in the rural areas. The main issue in both town and
country was the revitalisation of the ancient system of grammar
schools, now often decayed and increasingly useless to the 'middle
classes' – or at least perceived as being so. The fact that, according to
their original statutes, still in force, these schools often now gave a free
education to the poorer classes was seen as an undesirable wastage of
valuable endowments, which might now be put to a 'better' purpose. It
was through reorganisation of the resources available in these
endowments (whose misuse – often scandalous – had already been
revealed by a Parliamentary inquiry early in the century),[29] that these
groupings saw the means of constructing a rational structure of
schooling to meet the requirements of different strata in the social
hierarchy.

In the 1840s and 1850s, when these movements were already under
way, England was only just beginning to emerge from the turbulence
of Chartism. The increasing prosperity of the 1850s, which affected
both the agricultural world and industry, was now leading to a period
of social stability which was to last, in general, to the mid-1880s. This,
then, was a suitable time to encourage the development of new
educational structures that could both go some way to meeting the
new pressures arising from occupational and political change, and at
the same time stabilise, or even reinforce, the emergent hierarchic
social structure.

It was at this period (the 1850s to 1860s), then, that these elements
began to pressurise succeeding governments, and Parliament generally,
to set up a Royal Commission of Inquiry into the endowed (grammar)
schools and the private and 'proprietary' schools which had come into
being in large numbers to meet the new demands. This initiative had
already been preceded by Commissions investigating other areas – the
ancient universities, the 'public' schools and the elementary schools.[30]
With the appointment and report of the Schools Inquiry Commission

d the Act which followed it (1869), the basis had been laid for the reform of education for the middle and upper classes. The seal would be set on the total system with the passage of the Elementary Education Act one year later, in 1870. The blueprint for mid-century restructuring was now complete.

The Schools Inquiry Commission

Although the Schools Inquiry Commission (SIC) was the last of the Commissions that reported between 1850 and 1870 to be appointed, it may be convenient to deal with it first since it was directly concerned with the secondary education of the middle classes or middle strata. This Commission, as is well known, had the brief of examining all schools lying between the 'great' (or 'public') schools (which had already been investigated by the Clarendon Commission) and the elementary schools on which the Newcastle Commission had reported in 1861. Its proposals provide a classic example of what Ringer defines as 'vertical segmentation'.

The proposals, which cannot be considered here in any detail, were concerned to establish three grades of school, each designed for a specific level among the middle classes. In order to free resources for this restructuring, the Commission proposed to put an end once and for all to free education (an age-old right in many schools) and so to exclude the poor or working class. The proposals also involved putting an end to class-mixing (or heterogeneity) in the schools' intake (several had traditionally recruited students from different social strata) in order to develop a differentiated system of schools, each with a different leaving age and different curricula. With the object partly of sugaring the pill, provision was to be made from the endowments for a limited number of scholarships (or exhibitions) in the higher-grade schools which might be won by working-class or artisans' children in the lower (third) grade, thus building into the system a procedure allowing a strictly limited degree of social mobility.

The Commission was very clear that their primary objective was to bring some order into the work of the schools they examined. The schools 'need to have their work defined and then to be kept to that work', they reported. 'Each type of school should have its own proper aim set before it, and should be put under such rules as will compel it to keep to that aim.'[31] Their view was that sets of schools at different levels, or grades, needed to be created to serve different sections of the so-called 'middle-classes'. These are defined as the 'upper middle class', the 'middle middle class' and the 'lower middle class' (with which the Commission was particularly concerned).

In terms of the differentiated curricula proposed, first-grade schools were to focus on classical studies, both Latin and Greek. While second- and third-grade schools were both to teach Latin, only in first-grade schools could Greek be taught. As Greek was an essential requirement for entry to both Oxford and Cambridge at that time, this effectively restricted entry to these universities to pupils who attended first-grade schools. This recommendation appears as a piece of overt political (or social) engineering: it was during the last half of the century that the 'public' (and first-grade) schools almost entirely monopolised entry to Oxford and Cambridge.[32]

First-grade schools were to serve the upper middle and professional classes which the Commission defines as, first, those with large unearned incomes, along with successful professional men and business men, 'whose profits put them on the same level', and second, clergy, doctors, lawyers and the poorer gentry, who 'have nothing to look to but education to keep their sons on a high social level' (an interesting premonition of the concept of cultural capital).[33] In fact, several locally endowed schools investigated by the SIC were already developing as 'public, schools in the 1860s – for instance, Oundle, Uppingham and Repton – and some of the schools in the SIC's first grade became part of the revitalised 'public' school system in the period under review. First-grade schools were for children who would stay until the age of eighteen.

The second grade of school proposed was for children who left school at sixteen; these were day schools (not boarding) which, it was proposed, would prepare pupils for the army, the medical and legal professions, civil engineering, business and commercial life. It was envisaged that these should be patronised largely by the mercantile and trading classes – defined as larger shopkeepers, rising men of business and substantial tenant farmers. Latin would be included in the curriculum, as already indicated, but not Greek. Otherwise the curriculum would be modernised to include English literature, political economy, mathematics and science.[34] Here, then, was a deliberate attempt to meet the needs of the lesser bourgeoisie.

The third grade of school was designed for those leaving at fourteen, for 'a class distinctly lower in the scale', that is for smaller tenant farmers, small tradesmen and superior artisans. The establishment of efficient schools on this level was, the SIC held, of first importance. Their curriculum should (significantly) also include 'the elements of Latin' or a foreign language, English, history, elementary mathematics, geography and science. No one should be permitted to stay beyond fourteen.[35] It is worth noting the special attention given to the creation of third-grade schools in the light of the clear objective of attaching, by this means, the petty bourgeoisie and the upper working class firmly to their social superiors in the renovated grammar school system, and so isolating them from the working class with whom in the past (for example, the Chartist period and earlier, and in the 1860s franchise agitation) they had formed a sometimes powerful and threatening alliance.

The proposal to abolish free education, which was certainly implemented, involved charging sometimes quite substantial fees. It was proposed that these should also be graded, the highest, of course, being those for the first-grade schools, the lowest for third-grade ones.

Such was the neat, highly differentiated scheme proposed by the SIC. One thing that is certain, however, is that this scheme was not brought in in the pure form here proposed. No central or regional authority was set up to mastermind this reconstruction, as proposed in the Report. Instead, three Endowed Schools Commissioners were appointed, under the Act which followed the Report, with executive powers to implement reorganisation school by school, using the SIC Report as a guide to classifying individual schools. After five years, as a result of a Tory-Church backlash to their reforming activities, these powers were made over to the Charity Commission (a government office established in 1853). But statutory authority continued to be exercised, if now in a muted form, and on this basis change took place along the lines proposed in the Report. A new statutory basis for most of the endowed grammar schools was established during the thirty years following the 1869 Act, and to some extent these accorded with the Commission's proposals. Precisely how far this was the case we do not know, as this period has not, as yet, been effectively researched.[36] There is a great deal that needs doing to sort out how things actually developed during these years.

We have dealt so far with the middle strata and the proposals for educational reconstruction for this central grouping in the mid to late nineteenth century; but this period also saw what may be regarded as a classic case of systematisation with a clear class significance: the evolution of the independent or so-called 'public' schools as a cohesive, organic and self-contained grouping having the closest links with the ancient universities, and through this route with government (both Parliamentary and the civil service). The system that evolved, again partly as a result of state intervention, is unique to England and still obtains, though it may be said that in the last forty years or so it has lost something of its pre-eminence.

The 'public' schools developed as a 'system' in the period from 1860 to 1900. The Clarendon Commission, which reported on the leading 'great' schools in 1864, laid the basis for this development – for the reinvigoration and 'reform' of the traditional schools, which formed the core of the system. These were now, however, joined by the aspiring first-grade schools that the SIC had reported on, as well as by schools newly founded on their model.

The system of 'public' schools, as it developed in the closing years of the century, was of course entirely independent of the state, at least in a formal sense. These schools received no financial support directly from the state, were generally governed by a variety of (now reformed) semi-public, semi-private bodies, and were profoundly concerned to preserve this independence. When we speak of a 'system' of 'public' schools, it must be understood that this had no formal existence, except that the heads met together and organised the Headmasters' Conference, which had been brought into being in 1869 to defend the 'public' schools, 'in their hour of danger' as one headmaster put it,[37] that is, the danger of being taken over by the state, which was now becoming increasingly subject to popular pressure as a result of the extension of the franchise in 1867. These schools did, however, form close links with each other, as Honey has shown, thus reinforcing a hierarchy, with the most prestigious, such as Eton and Harrow, at the top, and the least prestigious, for instance Dover College, at the bottom.[38] No doubt each level within the total system could be characterised in terms of the social origin of their pupils and their occupational level after leaving school. As mentioned earlier, very close links were maintained with the individual colleges at Oxford and Cambridge, which were also independent foundations.

These schools played a key role in the symbiosis, or fusion, of the industrial and commercial (and financial) bourgeoisie and the aristocracy, together with leading elements from the liberal professions, into what is called the Victorian upper middle class. Having a high social status, they *conferred* that status on their pupils where these did not come from the gentry and the aristocracy. To have been educated at a 'public' school became, by the close of the century, the *sine qua non* for most leading positions in society, government, the civil service, law, the Church and the professions generally – and it was to these callings that many sons of industrialists now aspired. This, then, was a process which evolved as the industrial middle class began to demand a 'public' school education for their sons in place of the system of apprenticeship, family connections and the like which they had still relied on at mid-century.[39]

It is difficult to find any direct relationship between these schools and developing industry. In a sense these schools, even those specifically patronised by industrialists, turned their backs on industry and scarcely recognised it. Situated normally in remote rural areas, the schools pursued the ideal of a kind of country life-style in which games and the worship of athletics increasingly dominated from the 1860s on.[40] The central focus of studies, as recommended by the Clarendon Commission, remained the classics; modern studies, though now included, were given little time or prestige and remained peripheral. The 'hidden' curriculum was concerned not so much with cognitive (intellectual) development (though here there were exceptions) as with the development of character – reliability, conformity, honesty, courage, integrity – the sort of qualities, perhaps, that were now required of the governing caste in a rapidly developing imperialism. Some historians now ascribe England's economic difficulties in the second half of the twentieth century to what now appears as the deliberate rejection of science and technology (and of concern with industry) in the leading schools and universities in the late nineteenth century.[41]

Reverting to the Marxist model discussed earlier, it is difficult to make a case for a direct relationship between economic development and industry, and the nature and content of 'public' school education in the late nineteenth century. Clearly these were important institutions in terms of underpinning the social order, but their relations with industry were tangential, to say the least. Those schools that were popular with the industrial bourgeoisie in the north of England, for instance Uppingham and Radley (the latter established by a group of business men), developed similar lifestyles to the ancient schools which they took as their model – a classical education together with games and athletics. The whole inner structure of these schools, largely boarding, with 'houses', pastoral care by the teachers (as a primary and important function), the system of prefects and fags, and so on, had evolved over a long period and was by now both general and adapted to the perceived requirements of the period in terms of educational outcomes. These were now 'total institutions' (in the sociological sense), providing a very carefully controlled and structured environment as the means of induction for the upper middle-class young. Their role was social and political rather than economic.

Is there a stronger case, to move to the other end of the social spectrum, for arguing a direct relationship between the provision of universal elementary education and the economic requirements of mid-century? A Royal Commission had also investigated this area (the Newcastle Commission), reporting in 1861, but in this case the key legislation was postponed until 1870 (and succeeding Acts to 1880), when a compromised but widely supported system, involving a degree of local finance and control, was finally brought into being.

Certainly it is generally acknowledged that economic considerations were one factor leading to this measure – in particular the perennial argument that England was being overtaken, in terms of industrial and technological developments, by Prussia, France, Switzerland and other European countries, most of which had already established systems of universal compulsory elementary education well before England. The relatively poor showing of the British exhibits at the Paris Exhibition of 1867 was adduced as evidence of this. It was also argued, by manufacturers in the mid-1860s, that universal education was required in order to select, from the mass of the workers, those who, responding well to schooling, would make good foremen on the shop floor. But a close study seems to suggest that the centrally accepted motivation for this measure was not so much economic as directly political. This relates to the successful struggle of the labour movement and the radical bourgeoisie for the extension of the franchise, as shown by their relative success in 1867 – and with the likelihood of a further extension in the not too distant future.

In England measures concerning popular education in the nineteenth century were often specifically related to the extension of the franchise. It was the radical bourgeoisie (or rather, its ideological spokesmen) who first deliberately developed this policy in the early years of the century – as the means by which the industrial and commercial middle class might oust the traditional governing classes and achieve political power, in the early nineteenth century monopolised by Whigs and Tories, the two 'factions', as James Mill put it, of the aristocracy.[42]

How could this situation be transformed? Only by the massive extension of the franchise would it be possible for the middle class (bourgeoisie) to gain control of Parliament and overturn the rule of the aristocracy (or landed interest). But, if the working class were given the vote, would they not then have the power to overturn the existing social order in their own interests ('the world turned upside down')?

Hence the solution, strongly argued from the 1820s on by Mill and Bentham, the philosophic radicals: educate the masses; enlighten them; let them understand that their true interests lay in uniting with capital both economically and politically; let them understand the laws of political economy – especially the iron law of wages.

So the advanced industrial bourgeoisie favoured, on the one hand, the extension of the franchise to all males (in Bentham's case females as well), together with a massive extension of popular education. We have seen that, in the 1840s and 1850s, Cobden and other liberal manufacturers threw their weight strongly behind the mass provision of popular education.

Popular demand for the extension of the franchise reached a new peak in the mid-1860s. In 1867 three days of demonstrations in Hyde Park swung the issue. The Tory government of the day now conceded an extension of the franchise, so bringing a million artisans (or skilled workers) on to the voting registers for the first time. Robert Lowe's famous remark, 'I believe it will be absolutely necessary to compel our future masters to learn their letters', encapsulates the view that he and others now held.[43] Now was the time for a serious extension of popular education. The last two or three years of the 1860s saw a sudden consensus around the issue of the provision of universal elementary education. This seems to indicate that the 1870 Act was a *political*, rather than an economic, necessity.

So there was constructed, at the close of the crucial decision-making period – building, of course, on earlier developments – another level of schooling, again for a specific class (the working class, as written into the Act itself), which was largely self-contained and had no organic relationship at that time with the other levels of schooling now being brought into being.

The Emergent 'System'

Whatever the intentions, the outcomes of the mid-century educational reorganisation in England are clear enough: three main levels of schooling came into being in the period 1860 to 1900.

First, a cohesive grouping of 'public' schools for the upper middle class. Second, elementary schooling for the working class. The first of these was 'independent' of, but closely woven into, the state. The second was directly controlled and financed by the state, though in 'partnership' with the new local authorities (School Boards) and the voluntary bodies (the Churches).

At the same time, a third set of schools was brought into being, with the aim of restructuring education for the middle strata (or class) on three levels. The outcome, then, was the establishment of a highly differentiated system in which each level served, in theory at least, a specific social class (or subsection of a class), with each having a specific function.

In this situation the struggle between classes expressed itself in different ways. For instance, the early socialist and Chartist movements' concept of the content and character of popular education (as defined, for instance, in Lovett's *Chartism* in 1841) was very different from that of the system finally imposed. Again, the perspectives embraced historically by the industrial and commercial middle class, partly for reasons discussed earlier, differed radically from the nature and content of middle-class education as actually imposed, even if there was some acceptance of modernising tendencies.

The system that was imposed, in the period of reorganisation, was precise and neat, involving clear forms of differentiation (or segmentation); but there were many loose ends. Indeed by the 1890s it erupted in crisis, but this represents a new phase in developments.

To conclude, the reorganisation of education in England in the mid to late nineteenth century resulted in the construction of a highly differentiated system comprising several levels of schooling, differentiated in terms of curriculum, fees, length of school life and ethos. Each level was intended to cater for a specific section of the social spectrum. The resultant structure both reflected, and fed back into and so perpetuated, the existing social structure.

These developments do not bear out a strict reproduction model of the relations between education and society, as elaborated, for instance, by Bourdieu in relation to contemporary systems, since such a model (admittedly highly theoretical and challenging) cannot explain change. Yet the period from 1860 to 1900 was a period of rapid change, both in society *and* in education. How can a reproduction model account for the fusion, or symbiosis, of aristocracy and bourgeoisie, as cemented through the 'public' schools, which had the clear function of promoting such a fusion? Only, perhaps, if one accepts that the reproduction of social hierarchies may take different forms; and that this development in a sense simply meant that new means were found to ensure the, otherwise insecure, perpetuation of existing class relations.

Nor do developments in England bear out a linear model of the relationship between education and economic development. Indeed, economic developments appear in this period to have little direct relation with educational change. Later in the century, in the later 1880s and 1890s in particular, the new universities established in the provincial cities apparently responded more directly to economic requirements than any institutions in the period of restructuring. Changes in the 'base' (forces of production) certainly affected education indirectly (as argued at the start of this chapter) through urbanisation and population growth, and through the consequent emergence of a complex occupational pattern, particularly affecting the middle strata. But educational restructuring was not spearheaded by those representing economic or industrial interests and developments. Rather, this role was played, at a crucial phase, by those representing the aristocracy and gentry, who were concerned to preserve social stability and reinforce emerging social hierarchies.

The English experience, then, tends to the conclusion that education has a large degree of autonomy from the economic base. The forces primarily involved in restructuring and systematisation are political and social rather than economic. Gramsci's analysis, relating to hegemony and the role of civic society, seems central to an understanding of these developments. Unlike the French Marxist Althusser, Gramsci fully accepts that education can be a site of struggle between classes with different objectives and that the struggle of subordinate classes for hegemony may conflict with the role of 'established' culture. It is along these lines, I suggest, that educational developments in England at this time may best be interpreted.[44]

Notes

[1] Brian Simon, *The Two Nations and the Educational Structure, 1780-1870*, first published as *Studies in the History of Education, 1780-1870* (London, 1960), esp. chapter 6, pp227-336.
[2] *Ibid*.
[3] For instance, Henry Craik, *The State in its Relation to Education* (London, 1882) and later books in this genre.

[4] Sheila Fletcher, *Feminists and Bureaucrats: A Study in the Development of Girls' Education in the Nineteenth Century* (Cambridge, 1980).

[5] Such Executive Commissioners were appointed by the Acts concerning both Oxford and Cambridge, the 'public' or 'great' schools, and the endowed grammar schools.

[6] Reference will be made to 'England' rather than 'Britain' throughout. Scottish developments differed from English ones and need a separate study, but see Walter Humes and Hamish Paterson (eds.), *Scottish Culture and Scottish Education, 1800-1980* (Edinburgh, 1983). There were also important differences in Wales, relating in particular to the Welsh Intermediate Education Act of 1889. See Leslie Wynne Evans, *Studies in Welsh Education* (Cardiff, 1974).

[7] Geoffrey Holmes, *Augustan England. Professions, State and Society, 1680-1730* (London, 1982).

[8] For legal judgements affecting education, see David Owen, *English Philanthropy, 1660-1960* (Oxford, 1964). See also Simon, *The Two Nations*, esp. pp104-9.

[9] Schools Inquiry Commission (Taunton), *Report*, vol. 1 (1868), p93.

[10] Geoffrey Best, *Mid-Victorian Britain, 1851-1875* (London, 1973), p170.

[11] Harold Perkin, *The Origins of Modern English Society, 1780-1880* (London, 1969), p302.

[12] Samuel Bowles and Herbert Gintis, *Schooling in Capitalist America* (London, 1976).

[13] Pierre Bourdieu and Jean-Claude Passeron, *Reproduction in Education, Society and Culture* (London and Beverly Hills, 1977).

[14] Joan Simon, *Education and Society in Tudor England* (Cambridge, 1966); Foster Watson, *The English Grammar Schools to 1660: Their Curriculum and Practice* (Cambridge, 1908), pp530ff.

[15] Brian Simon, *The Two Nations*, chapter 1, pp17-71; for the Manchester College of Arts and Science and the Manchester Academy, see pp58-62. For the Lunar Society, see Robert E Schofield, *The Lunar Society of Birmingham* (Oxford, 1963).

[16] Of the 14 members of the Lunar Society, 4 (Richard Edgeworth, Thomas Day, Erasmus Darwin and Joseph Priestley) published important books on education.

[17] Jeremy Bentham, *Chrestomathia* (London, 1816); Brian Simon, *The Two Nations*, pp79-82.

[18] This movement is interestingly analysed in Ian Inkster and Jack Morrell (eds.), *Metropolis and Province: Science in British Culture, 1780-1850* (London, 1983). See especially the introductory chapter by Inkster and the chapters by Orange (on Newcastle) and Neve (on Bristol).

[19] W D Rubinstein, 'Wealth, Elites and the Class Structure of Modern Britain', *Past and Present*, No 76 (August 1977). Rubinstein's thesis concerning the 'two middle classes' is very relevant to this analysis, but see also W D Rubinstein, *Capitalism, Culture, and Decline in Britain 1750-1990* (London, 1993). G R Searle, in *Entrepreneurial Politics in Mid-Victorian Britain* (Oxford, 1993) concludes his chapter on education by claiming that the entrepreneurial Radicals 'failed to put together a distinctive educational

programme. Indeed, in few areas of public life was their failure so palpable' (p270). Both Rubinstein's and Searle's books were published after this essay was written.

20 Gladstone's letter to the Clarendon Commission is reprinted in the *Report of the Public School Commission*, vol. 2, pp42-3: 'The materials of what we call classical training were prepared, and we have a right to say were advisedly and providentially prepared, in order that it might become ... the complement of Christianity in its application to the culture of the human being.'

21 Introduction to the English edition of *Socialism: Utopian and Scientific*, in Karl Marx and Frederick Engels, *Selected Works* (London, 1950), vol. 2 pp102-3.

22 Michael Sanderson's *The Universities and British Industry, 1870–1970* (London, 1972), a full specialist study, makes it clear that it was not until the later 1880s or 1890s that the universities, both ancient and modern, began to make any substantial contribution to British industry.

23 Elie Halévy, in *Imperialism and the Rise of Labour* (London, 1961), gives the following figures for British capital invested abroad: 1842, £144 million; 1877, £600 million; 1882, £875 million; 1893, £1698 million; 1905, £2025 million.

24 Though it could be argued that Herbert Spencer's *Education, Intellectual, Moral and Physical*, first published in 1861, which restated and developed the utilitarian approach, came close to such a statement, while T.H. Huxley also wrote much on education from an advanced liberal–scientific standpoint in the closing decades of the century.

25 Donald Jones, *The Making of the Educational System, 1851–81* (London, 1977), includes a useful analysis of this movement in chapter 2, pp13-27.

26 David Allsobrook, 'An Investigation of Precedents for the Recommendations of the Schools Inquiry Commission, 1864-1867', unpublished PhD thesis, University of Leicester, 1979. See especially chapter 3, 'Local Authorities and Unilateralism: I, Mid-Century Contrast: Diocesan and County Boards: County Schools'. See also David Allsobrook, *Schools for the Shires* (Manchester, 1986).

27 For the influence of this grouping, the 'academic liberals', see David Reeder (ed.), *Educating Our Masters* (Leicester, 1980), especially the editor's introduction. See also chapter 6 – T.H. Green's 1882 lecture concerning the aspirations of middle-class intellectuals of the 1860s to develop a national system of education based on the reform of middle-class schools.

28 Allsobrook, 'An Investigation', chapters 3 and 7.

29 *First, Second and Third Reports of the Commissioners on the Education of the Poor, 1819-20*.

30 Royal Commission on Oxford University (established 1850); Royal Commission on Cambridge University (1850); Royal Commission on Elementary Education (Newcastle Commission, 1858); Royal Commission on the Public Schools (Clarendon Commission, 1861). The Schools Inquiry Commission (Taunton Commissions) was appointed in 1864, reporting in 1868.

31 Schools Inquiry Commission, *Report*, Vol 1, pp576, 578.

32 An investigation of a sample of Cambridge students shows that the

proportion coming from grammar schools fell from 16 per cent in the period 1752-99 to 7 per cent in the period 1850-99. Of the remaining 93 per cent in the latter period, 82 per cent came from 'public' schools and 11 per cent from private schools. See Hester Jenkins and D Caradog Jones, 'Social Class of Cambridge Alumni', *British Journal of Sociology*, Vol 1, No 2 (June 1950).

[33] Schools Inquiry Commission, *Report*, Vol 1, pp16, 18.

[34] *Ibid.*, Vol 1, p20.

[35] *Ibid.*

[36] But see Owen, *English Philanthropy*, chapter 9, 'Remodelling Ancient Trusts: The Endowed Schools'; and Fletcher, *Feminists and Bureaucrats*, for a thorough study of the outcomes of the Commissioners' work for girls' education.

[37] G R Parkyn, *Life and Letters of Edward Thring* (London, 1900), p178.

[38] John Honey, 'Tom Brown's Universe: The Nature and Limits of the Victorian Public Schools Community', in Brian Simon and Ian Bradley (eds.), *The Victorian Public School* (Dublin, 1975), pp19-33.

[39] Rubinstein makes the point that it was the London-based commercial and financial section of the middle class, mainly anglican, which was 'far readier to send its sons to a major public school and Oxbridge, than were the manufacturers [from the Midlands and the North]'. See Rubinstein, 'Wealth, Elites', pp113-14.

[40] See Norman Vance, 'The Ideal of Manliness'; and J A Mangan, 'Athleticism: A Case Study of the Evolution of an Educational Ideology', in Simon and Bradley (eds.), *The Victorian Public School*, chapters 7 and 9.

[41] This position is strongly argued in Martin J. Wiener, *English Culture and the Decline of the Industrial Spirit, 1850-1980* (Cambridge, 1981).

[42] For an analysis of Mill's position, see Simon, *The Two Nations*, pp74-9.

[43] A Patchett Martin, *Life and Letters of the Right Honourable Robert Lowe Viscount Sherbrooke* (London, 1893), Vol 2, p323. To the leading liberals 'this remark was no more than a truism', as James Bryce put it. See Reeder, *Educating Our Masters*, p8.

[44] L Althusser, 'Ideology and Ideological State Apparatuses', in L Althusser, *Lenin and Philosophy and Other Essays* (London, 1971), pp121-73. For Antonio Gramsci's position, see his *Prison Notebooks*, ed. and trans. Quintin Hoare and Geoffrey Nowell Smith (London, 1971).

3: Cushioning Reform: the Role of Executive Commissioners in the Re-structuring of Education in Mid-Nineteenth Century*

No one working in education in England today can fail to be conscious of a large state apparatus – or bureaucracy. Until recently one had only to wander up York Street, on the south bank of the Thames, to be made aware of its size – Elizabeth House, the headquarters of what was then the Department of Education and Science, is a massive building occupying the whole length of the street and, with the Shell headquarters on the other side, symptomatic of the concrete jungles characteristic of modern urban development. It seems a far cry from the relatively civilised ambience of Curzon Street, and certainly from Belgrave Square, the headquarters of many years ago. The habitat of this bureaucracy is not only spatially visible, its operations across the

* This essay was first drafted several years ago. The headquarters of the Department of Education has recently been transferred to Sanctuary Buildings in Whitehall. I have, however, deliberately retained the original opening paragraph, since it accurately reflects the stress I wished to place on the trend towards centralisation of control. Since this essay was drafted, this has, of course, been greatly extended.

whole field of education appear ubiquitous. In the last few years (early 1970s) it has moved energetically into higher education, playing a directing role, for instance, in relation to the re-organisation of teacher education – of a controversial kind inconceivable in the past. It is clear that the degree and level of state intervention is now rapidly increasing, and that this tendency will not easily be diverted.

The purpose of this essay is to look carefully at a specific phase of state intervention in education in the past. It seems generally held that, in the nineteenth century, such initiatives in England were confined to the elementary sphere, and in relation to this historians have concentrated on the growth of the Education Department (established in 1839) so that attention has tended to focus on this aspect only. There is a long tradition behind this approach; for instance, J. E. G. de Montmorency, in his book on this topic (*State Intervention in English Education*, 1902), though dealing with large issues (such as the Reformation and education) in the earlier period, finishes with several chapters focussing on elementary education as marking the apotheosis of state intervention. This tradition was carried on in books such as Marjorie Cruickshank's *Church and State in English Education* (1963) and James Murphy's *Church, State and Schools in Britain, 1800-1970* (1971), together with more recent publications. Yet in point of fact, the state intervened in education across the board in the nineteenth century (and, in some instances, considerably earlier). Indeed I have already put the thesis that the crucial 'moment of change' in English education as a whole was the period 1850 to 1870. But there was no Elizabeth House then, only a relatively small department under the aegis of the Committee of Council. How then were the sometimes considerable changes in school and university education (other than elementary) accomplished? What machinery was used to ensure that planned objectives were realised? What part was played in the pre-planning, behind the scenes, in Parliament, and by what means were executive or administrative actions ensured? These are important questions and it is on these I intend to concentrate.

In the period 1850 to 1870, as already indicated, state institutions became closely involved in the restructuring of English education. The technique used – and this covers the universities, the 'great' schools, as well as the endowed schools – was in all cases similar. This can be broken down into four, sometimes five stages. The first is that of effective Parliamentary action. In all the cases I refer to, this resulted in the appointment of a Royal Commission of Enquiry. The actual membership of these Commissions was clearly of major importance to the Government, which normally had a fairly clear idea as to what outcome they desired. Some people selected themselves, as it were, but naturally a good deal of care was given to selecting the right men (sic), not to speak of intrigue and manoeuvring. There is a great deal of research to be done on what might be called the politics of these Commissions, of the kind that David Allsobrook has pioneered in relation to the Taunton (Schools Inquiry) Commission and Colin Shrosbree for the Clarendon (Public Schools) Commission.[1]

The second stage is, of course, the actual enquiry carried through by the Royal Commission, culminating in the publication of a report plus evidence, including recommendations for action. Once the Commission has reported, it must be remembered, it goes out of existence. Neither the report nor its recommendations can be taken as having been carried out in practice, as has sometimes been the tendency, for instance, in relation to the Schools Inquiry Commission's recommendations about the three grades of endowed grammar schools. Nevertheless the report and the recommendations are there, awaiting, as it were, further action, and at that time there was certainly an expectation that action would follow; these Royal Commissions were not pigeon-holing devices.

The third stage is again that of Parliamentary action. In the case of each of the four Commissions I am concerned with (on Oxford, Cambridge, the public and the endowed schools), a period of discussion and debate followed the publication of the reports of the Commissions, in all cases leading to legislative action. So we have the Acts relating to Oxford and Cambridge, passed in 1854 and 1856, that relating to the public schools passed in 1868 (four years after the Commission had reported), and that relating to the endowed schools in 1869. It is possible that the dating of the two latter Acts, so close to that of 1870 concerning elementary education, accounts to some extent for their relative neglect by educational historians, though David Allsobrook and Colin Shrosbree have begun to fill this gap with their recent studies.

These Acts laid down certain legislative principles which now became the law of the land. For instance, the Endowed Schools Act abolished the Master's freehold in his appointment, a situation which has been under very strong attack for decades. Again, the Oxford University Act abolished the Hebdomadal Board, and defined and substituted a reconstituted Hebdomadal Council. However each of these Acts contained clauses to which I wish to draw very special attention. In each case Executive Commissioners were appointed with statutory powers to ensure that certain crucially important actions were carried out in line with the broad principles defined in the Acts themselves. For instance, the very first clause of the Oxford University Act names the Commissioners whose job it was to carry through many of the principal reforms proposed in the Royal Commission's report; primarily to ensure that the statutes of colleges and university were formulated on new principles. Those appointed under the Public Schools Act were charged with ensuring that the new governing bodies were brought into being again in line with the principles laid down in the Act. The responsibilities of these commissioners were many and varied and I will be discussing them later on.

The four stages I have outlined normally formed the cycle of state intervention. Nevertheless there was a fifth stage which could be added to the procedures outlined above. This involved the appointment of Parliamentary select committees to investigate the working of the Acts. This technique was used in the case of the Endowed Schools Act in particular, as is well known, first in 1873 and again later. Select Committees were used on other occasions but in these cases they should be regarded simply as part of the Parliamentary action outlined under stage three. For instance, during the four years of discussion about legislation following the report of the public schools commission, which involved the introduction of three Bills, all abortive, select committees were appointed both by the Lords and the Commons to investigate key issues further and to make proposals about the Bills to be presented to Parliament.

I propose now to focus attention on the procedures relating to Commissioners appointed under these Acts. These Commissioners clearly operated as agents of the state – or, perhaps, as embryo civil servants – charged with *statutory powers* to ensure institutional change as determined by the Act. It seemed to me that there might be some interest in extracting these particular historically obscure and neglected groups, or agents, for what can only be, in a short paper, a superficial examination. However, first, a brief glance at the politics of this procedure.

We may start with the public schools. Here it becomes at once apparent that the appointment of Executive Commissioners must be assessed as essentially a conservative move – or manoeuvre. This was pressed by those elements in the House of Lords who originally fought very strongly against any legislation at all following the report of the Clarendon Commission. Failing in this battle, Lords Derby and Stanhope fought for an Executive Commission as an alternative to *direct Parliamentary action* to establish new governing bodies for each of the public schools. The direct appointment by Parliament of these governing bodies was on the order of the day, so that the appointment of Executive Commissioners to carry out this task privately, as it were, and in close consultation with the schools themselves, was seen by the Conservatives as a means of saving these schools from the possible consequences of such direct action with the scope this would give for outside bodies to influence the results. Having achieved this objective, Conservative forces then directed their efforts to limiting the power of the Executive Commissioners as much as possible. In the outcome in this case they were at least partially successful. They secured their Executive Commissioners, who included the Marquis of Salisbury, already a leading Tory spokesman, as a token that no really radical changes would be brought about, but they did not succeed in limiting their powers to the extent they wanted. The essence of the Bill as finally passed was the power it accorded to the Executive Commissioners to *force* changes on the governing bodies. In the outcome the Executive Commissioners did reconstitute governing bodies on new lines, and insist on certain educational reforms, in particular ensuring that French, Mathematics and Science formed part of the normal school curriculum. These were both points, of course, which the Royal Commission itself had strongly recommended. It is worth noting, however, that although the Act was passed in 1868, it was 1870 before the seven schools concerned had their new sets of governors, and that only Winchester and Eton managed to arrange for these new bodies themselves (as they had the power to do before the Executive Commissioners' powers became operative). Another four years passed (1874) before the new statutes drawn up by the new sets of governors could be agreed upon (a total of *ten* years after the appointment of the Clarendon Commission).

An insight into the working of the Executive Commissioners can be gained from E. Graham's fascinating *The Harrow Life of Henry Montagu Butler* (1920). The main issues affecting Harrow that would have to be solved arising from the Public Schools Act were (i) the conditions of foundationers (freedom of the school), (ii) the number of home boarders, (iii) the continuation, or otherwise, of the English form (to which local tradesmen's sons were shunted). Statutes for the school covering these and other matters, drawn up by the new Governing Body, were approved in July 1874. The composition of the Governing Body was clearly crucial in determining these delicate and highly political questions, relation to the legalisation of the long process of alienation of that school from its locality, in its transition to public school status in the nineteenth century.

Since no statutes had been produced by the old Governing Body by the expiration of the time limit, the Executive Commissioners issued their own statues on 13th October 1870. These laid down the composition of the new Governing Body as follows – that this should be composed of ten persons, one elected by the Hebdomadal Council of Oxford, one by the Senate of Cambridge, one by the president and council of the Royal Society, one by the Lord Chancellor, one by the head and assistant masters, and five from the existing Governing Body. The new Governing Body set up by the Executive Commissioners, then, consisted of the following: James, second Duke of Verulam (Chairman), James, first Duke of Abercorn, John, fifth Earl Spencer, George, third Baron Northwick, and W. H. Stone Esq. These five had all been members of the old Governing Body of six (one peer stood down). The new Governors included Sir John Wickens, the Right Honourable Montague Bernard, Professor B. F. Westcott, Professor John Tyndall (the scientist), and C. F. Roundell, who was the Masters' choice.[2]

It was all seen that, within evident limitations, some new blood had been brought on to the Governing Body which now no longer consisted only of dukes, earls and barons, with one commoner. However Butler (the headmaster) found this group a comfortable body to deal with, and had no difficulty whatever in getting their support to regularise the *status quo*. The new Governing Body decided to establish the lower school of John Lyon, under their auspices, for 'a practical and liberal education suitable for boys, destined to trade and similar occupations'. Some of the endowment was set aside for this purpose, and this was the final action regularising the legal position of Harrow as an independent public school. Graham notes that 'Dr. Butler's memoranda and the entries in the Governors' minute book show how frequently his opinion had been consulted or proferred'. The new members of the Governing Body were likely, on the whole, to support the school's objective. Thus Butler writes to Westcott on his appointment, 'what a happy coincidence your little boy should arrive just when you become our sovereign'. This new body drew up the statutes for the school which were finally approved on 7th July 1874.[3]

It seems clear, then, that in relation to the Public Schools Act, the use of the executive Commissioners technique was, in effect, a means of bringing about a consensus change in a way least disruptive to the schools as they were then developing. Bishop, in *The Rise of a Central Authority for English Education* (1971) points to the fact that, in the late 1860s and 70s, 'what was possibly the last aristocratic government in English history created a closed system of schools for the governing class' (p237). If this is so, then one instrument bringing this about was certainly the Executive Commissioners, who played a key role at a crucial moment.

Let us now shift our attention to the universities, concentrating specifically on Oxford, since the real issues of university reform in the 1850s focus on this university rather than Cambridge. Here we have a complex institution, mediaeval in origin, consisting of a federation of independent, autonomous colleges, linked together into a university, in a situation where the colleges held most of the cards, and where the university was relatively powerless. Readers of Sir William Hamilton's brilliant, if vitriolic, attacks on Oxford in the *Edinburgh Review* in the 1830s will know very well the situation to which I am referring. One of the major sets of recommendations of the Oxford Commission, which reported in 1852, related specifically to this point. The Commission argued that the power of the university must be strengthened *vis-à-vis* the colleges, and made a number of recommendations to this effect.

The Oxford University Act of 1854 did, of course, lay down certain general principles. But to realise these in practice meant bringing each of the independent colleges into line. The situation was somewhat analagous to the issue, in 1965, of Circular 10/65 by the Labour government bringing in comprehensive education. This Circular, which of course had no legal sanction or statutory power, reflected an intention, but it early became clear that what mattered was which precise schemes for comprehensive reorganisation were accepted or rejected by the Minister (or DES) under the terms of the Circular. Shortly after its issue, supporters of comprehensive education in England were dismayed by the Minister's acceptance of the Doncaster scheme of 'guided parental choice' on the one hand (which seemed expressly designed to reinforce class differentiation), and the simultaneous rejection of the Liverpool scheme for all-through comprehensives (as a 'botched-up' scheme) on the other. It immediately became clear that, whatever was said in the Circular, the actual pattern of local school systems that developed would reflect the decisions made in each individual case. It was these decisions, therefore, that were of key importance.

Similarly the Oxford University Act of 1854 represented an intention, though having in this case statutory force. However here again what mattered were the precise changes brought about in the colleges by the Executive Commissioners appointed in the first clause, especially in the delicate area of college-university relations. Here Clause 38 is crucial. This laid down that the Commissioners must make due provision (i) for the wants of colleges and halls, and the advancement of religion and learning among their own members, and (ii) for aid towards the establishment of the professoriate 'on the enlarged basis in the several main branches of science and letters, and with adequate duties and emoluments, by appropriating portions of the divisible revenues of any college for that purpose ... especially where it appears to the Commissioners that the college is well able to make such provision'. College statutes also had to be amended in relation to closed fellowships, scholarships and, among other matters, to the university statutes concerning the government of the university. It was Clause 38 which really threatened these ancient closed corporations and held the key to an increase in the power and ability of the university as such to adapt its organisation to modern requirements relating, for instance, to science, technology and similar branches of study.

Clearly, therefore, very wide scope was left to the Executive Commissioners to determine outcomes. Their character, outlook and actions are evidently of crucial importance. But it is at this stage, in the actual selection of the Executive Commissioners, that we see the government now treating the colleges with kid gloves. There had, of course, been massive opposition to the appointment of the original royal Commission both in Parliament and, in particular, at the University of Oxford. This is well documented in the Commission's report. It is well known that many colleges refused to give evidence to the Commission, while the university as a whole (or rather, its governing body) appealed in the Privy Council against the right of Parliament to appoint a Royal Commission to investigate the university. The Executive Commissioners, on the other hand, were now given powers to *require* the production of documents, accounts, and information from both university and colleges. Further, no oath was now pleadable against giving such evidence.

It is interesting to note, then, that as W.R. Ward writes (in *Victorian Oxford*, 1965), 'the original names had been chosen with a view to minimising opposition in the university'. At the head of the Commissioners was the Earl of Ellesmere, a peer with Liberal inclinations. However he was balanced by the appointment of two distinguished lawyers with strong High Church sympathies – Mr Justice Coleridge and Sir John Awdry. The fourth member was the Bishop of Ripon, C.T. Longley, ex-student of Christ Church and (then) head of Harrow school, later to be Archbishop of Canterbury. Finally, there was appointed G.H.S. Johnson, Dean of Wells; this appointment was made as a sop to the Liberals in that one place, and one only, was thus given to a member of the original Royal Commission (whose composition and report were decidedly of a Liberal character). This last place, according to Ward, should have gone to the Bishop of Lincoln, Chairman of the original Commission. But he was ill, and in any case *persona non grata* at the university. The position therefore fell to Johnson, the man regarded by Pusey (High Church Conservative) as the 'least noxious' of the members of the Royal Commission. For the important posts of secretaries, a balance was maintained by appointing Goldwin Smith, a Liberal, and S.W. Wayte, fellow and tutor of Trinity College, and a member of the Conservative wing of the Oxford reformers.[4]

It might be thought that those who wanted the minimum change had been well looked after. Perhaps because of this the appointment of these Commissioners was met by a 'torrent of abuse' from the Liberals in Parliament. As a result two more were appointed, the ubiquitous Lord Harrowby, who played an important part in the Schools Inquiry Commission later, characterised by the *Guardian*, the Church of England newspaper, as 'a respectable peer', and Cornewall Lewis, similarly characterised as 'a clever laborious Whig'. However, before the Commissioners started work the latter resigned, to be replaced by Edward Twisleton, rationalist and Liberal. This appointment caused difficulties later which, unfortunately, we cannot go into here.

It already seems clear that the appointment of Executive Commissioners was, in this original case (previous to the Public Schools Act) a Conservative measure. Thus Jowett, in his correspondence with Gladstone about the Oxford University Bill, proposed that everything should be done by legislation, including the revision of both university and college statutes. Gladstone, still, of course, in his Tory period, opposed this. 'By means of a Commission', Gladstone wrote, 'Parliamentary reluctance may be softened ... a more complete and yet a somewhat milder measure accomplished – and the question thus rescued from the risk of the serious evils attending repeated Parliamentary interpositions'. To this Jowett replied that 'the great objection to a Commission is that it will work unjustly or it will not work at all. It will have to treat in detail and in a semi-legal manner matters which can only be treated by laying down a new general principle'. In the event, it is difficult not to agree that Jowett was correct. Without going into details, it is quite clear that the colleges were dealt with with the utmost consideration. Ward assesses their work as follows 'In the end the work of the Commission turned out as its composition had suggested from the beginning. With the aid of supplementary Acts the Commission completed its labours in 1858 to the applause of reformers of the High Church kind'. The *Guardian* commended their labours. There cannot be a doubt, it wrote, 'that they have performed a very considerable work, and on the whole well; that, without compromising the main principles of the Act of Parliament, they have dealt tenderly with the colleges; that their spirit has been Conservative and conciliatory; that they have laboured to reform, not to root up; to invigorate, not to revolutionise, the Oxford system'. It is true that they did succeed in 'wheedling' from unwilling colleges a number of professorial endowments – nevertheless the existing balance between colleges and university was not upset, in spite of the Royal Commission's report and the Act. Certainly the more forward looking Liberal reformers were much disappointed. Thus in Mark Pattison's view, the partial opening of foundations did a great amount of good but, he adds, 'this sweeping away of local claims was nearly all the good that the Commission of 1854 effected. After all the contention about the professoriate what the Commission did in this direction was without method – crude, sporadic'.

Without itemising the changes that were brought about through this method, one thing is perfectly clear. That is, that the 1850 Commission, and the legislation following it, together with the actions of the Executive Commissioners, by no means solved the basic problems of the university. All these issues rose again in sharpened form some twenty years later, when a second Royal Commission investigated both Oxford and Cambridge. Once again the technique of appointing Executive Commissioners was resorted to in the Act passed in 1877. Once again these Commissioners, appointed by a Tory government now headed by Lord Salisbury, were a pretty backward-

looking lot. They included Lord Selbourne who, as Roundell Palmer
had often pleaded the case of the Church at Oxford, Lord Redesdale
(characterised by Ward as 'obstructive') and J.W. Burgon (regarded as
the buffoon of Oxford catholicism)! The report and the Act which
followed had given a high priority, even more than in the 1850s, to
reforming the college-university connection. Nevertheless, once again,
this technique resulted in the colleges being treated with the very greatest
consideration. The Act gave the colleges a given time to prepare their
own schemes, and further made the extraordinary concession that each
college would have three representatives on the Commission as actual
voting members when their own statutes were being drawn up. In
practice, once again (as Ward put it), the Executive Commissioners
'were for the most part content to follow the wishes of the colleges'
representatives'. Ward's assessment of the Commission is that it 'settled
none of the problems which had led to its appointment'. He continues, 'a
generation later when Lord Curzon as Chancellor took up the question
of university reform, the old issues of the relations of the university and
the colleges, and of university extension, the old Liberal grievances
against the university constitution and the inadequate endowment of
research, were still being agitated'. All sorts of anomalies arose about the
revenues of colleges, and their ability to subsidise the universities'
revenues. Nor could these defects be blamed on the fact that the
Commission had no idea of the size of the revenue of which it was
disposing (it did). The primacy of the college system was maintained as
the secret of Oxford's usefulness. In this sense, 'The heart of the
university remained untouched and able to adapt itself to the demands of
married fellows, and to the increased weight and variety of teaching for
the honours schools'. This is how Ward concludes his book.[5]

Today, over a hundred years later, the colleges appear still established
as the centre and focus of university life both at Oxford and Cambridge –
with their endowments, feasts, sinecure headships, and particular
relations with the 'public' and independent school system. I make no
comment on this, except to say that the reform of these two institutions,
using these methods over the last one hundred and fifty years, can
perhaps best be regarded as a highly successful enterprise in the preservation of traditionalism. Perhaps the most remarkable survival is that of
All Souls College, Oxford, with its fabled millions of pounds of
endowments and no undergraduate students at all; slightly bent by the
criticisms of Oxford's own Franks Commission more than twenty years
ago, it proudly survives today almost in its mediaeval form.[6]

Summing up so far, one might say that the ploy of the appointment of Executive Commissioners was *the* means by which the really decisive issues were taken out of the realm of public disputation and possible control. In the case of Oxford, there was first a Royal Commission report, highly critical, quite radical in parts, which reflected an important movement of public opinion, though its personnel was very carefully chosen. The publication of the report itself took some of the sting out of the issue. But something had to be done – in the end, legislation. With the passage of the Act, the matter was passed to the Executive Commissioners. By this means it was taken from the glare of publicity and effectively removed from Parliamentary control (though the statutes the Commissioners approved had admittedly to be laid before Parliament). The Executive Commissioners were themselves very carefully chosen. They had to be acceptable both to the institutions concerned and to Parliament, but, above all, they could not be radical. They took the crucial decisions. This analysis appears to apply both to the Oxford and Cambridge Commissioners of the 1850s and 1870s, and to those appointed under the Public Schools Act.

Can we, from these instances, draw a general conclusion to the effect that the appointment of Executive Commissioners always represents a Conservative technique for minimising the impact of change? Let us turn, briefly, to the fourth Royal Commission in our period, the Schools Inquiry Commission.

Here we have a very different situation. This Commission produced a sharp, almost ruthless report, compared to the others. It did not in any sense pull its punches. In the course of its enquiries, the Commission subjected all endowed grammar schools to detailed examination. Each school was visited by an Assistant Commissioner, and the twenty plus volumes of the report are concerned with material based on these visitations, usually containing definite proposals for each school. As is well known, the Commission proposed a thorough re-organisation of the endowed schools. It also proposed a whole administrative structure, including the setting up of provincial authorities with considerable powers, an examination system for these schools, and the raising of revenue from the schools to cover the costs.

The Royal Commission reported in 1868. The Endowed Schools Act which followed was put on the statute book in 1869 – only one year later. The original bill consisted of two parts, one of which contained all the most radical proposals of the Commission. As a result of negotiations and discussions, the part of the bill containing the more radical proposals was never proceeded with in Parliament. In spite of this, as is well known, the Act – or its outcome – ran into serious difficulties.

The Endowed Schools Act also provided for the appointment of Commissioners whose job it was to apply the intentions of the Act to individual schools. These Commissioners were given very wide powers indeed. Clause 9 empowered them to carry out 'the main design of the founders' by putting 'a liberal education in the reach of all'. It also gave them powers to alter, add to or make new trusts, directions, etc. relating to endowed schools. They were also accorded powers to alter governing bodies, while a number of detailed clauses set out what the schemes they were to bring into being might be concerned with. In point of fact, then, it was left to the Commissioners to implement the Act in practice in each individual case. The Act also provided for the appointment of Assistant Commissioners, clerks and so on – in fact an efficient office to enable the work to be done. That the extent of the work involved may have been underestimated seems clear from Clause 59, which limited the powers of the Commissioners until 31 December 1872 – or to 31 December 1873, if determined by Her Majesty in Council, by which time, presumably, it was expected the job would be done.

A distinctive feature in this case is that, unlike the previous Acts discussed, no Commissioners were named in the Act itself. Why was this?

One explanation may be that the Irish Church Bill was going through Parliament at the same time, and considerable public attention was focused on this. It appears that the Endowed Schools Act was almost smuggled through Parliament unawares! Certainly the debates relating to it appear somewhat supine, and it seems that members of Parliament did not recognise, or anticipate, the opposition that the Act would lead to. As for the appointment of Commissioners, it appears that Gladstone (now rapidly moving to a radical/Liberal position) did not want the Commissioners appointed in the Act itself as he realised that their character would determine its outcome, and if their names were announced and proved unacceptable, this might put in question the whole principle of the Bill which Gladstone wanted passed, but felt was too radical for the House of Commons. In a speech defending the lack of nominations in the Bill, Gladstone quoted a number of precedents, but referred to Acts not in the education sphere.[7]

In the outcome, the Endowed Schools Commissioners were

appointed by Order in Council. The Act limited these to three, and those appointed were Lord Lyttleton, Arthur Hobhouse and Canon H.G. Robinson. Lyttleton had been a member of the Royal Commission (Taunton). He had also been a member of the Clarendon Commission before that – and indeed he played a very important part in the whole restructuring of education in England in the mid-nineteenth century. He had a close connection with Gladstone, both having married sisters; he was a member of the National Society, and generally a very energetic man with strong views both about education and about endowments in particular.

As a member of the Church of England, Lyttleton was suspect to some people – before the Select Committee on the Endowed Schools Act in 1873 he had to defend himself and his colleagues against the accusation that membership of the Church of England was a necessary qualification for becoming a Commissioner.[8] But already in 1869 two of the Commissioners laid up a good deal of trouble for themselves by expressing publicly very definite views on the question as to how they intended to handle endowments. Hobhouse revealed what his opinions were in a paper he delivered to the Social Science Association in that year. 'To talk of the piety or benevolence of the people who give property to public uses', he had said, 'is a misuse of language springing from confusion of ideas. As a matter of fact, I believe, as I have said elsewhere at more length', he went on, 'that donors to public uses are less under the guidance of reason and conscience, and more under the sway of baser passions, than other people'.[9] In dealing with charities, 'the first principle is that the public should not be compelled to take whatever is offered to it ... the second principle is that the grasp of the dead hand should be taken off absolutely and finally'. Lyttleton said, in the discussion following the paper, that if he and Hobhouse were permitted freedom of action, 'the pious founders would go to the wall'. The subsequent actions of the Commissioners in any case where they took radical measures only confirmed the violent impression formed by these words.

Clearly these were Commissioners who meant business. Together with their seven Assistant Commissioners, they managed to formulate 317 schemes relating to different endowed schools in a period of four years, ninety-seven of which had been placed before Parliament. In their report to the Committee of Council in 1872, the Endowed School Commissioners listed what had been achieved by that time. In reporting this they added that the work so far accomplished was only a small proportion of that which came within the scope of the Act. After dealing with the nature of their work under various headings, a section follows headed 'Magnitude of work as a whole'. This states clearly that 'it will also be readily seen what a number of years is required for the completion of a work by which each Endowment must have its separate Scheme; in which each Scheme must pass before, and satisfy at least, four different tribunals, and many Schemes must do more; and in which every species of interest is to be saved or compensated or duly regarded: not only pecuniary interests of living persons ... but those of indefinite classes and unborn generations, as to which there is no solid basis for judgment, and consequently an indefinite variety of opinion'.[10]

Their report, dated 21 February 1872, concludes 'our experience in attempting to work the Act has shown that the country was hardly prepared for its reception'. Any proposals of organic upheaval (like joining together endowments) was met with passionate resistance. They conclude 'in our case a wholly new machine has been set to work a law, of which a large proportion is new, and thereby to disturb a great number of interests, traditions and sentiments. And we have not had to wait till suitors come to us for assistance, but to take the initiative bringing the law to bear on them'. The Act was passed to deal with 'great and accumulated evils'. 'Now it has been passed, we cannot believe that it ought not to be administered in the spirit which dictated its provisions'.[11]

It is certainly true that the Commissioners evoked strong opposition for a number of reasons – particularly perhaps because of their secularising tendency, and because of the ruthless way they carried out their brief to abolish free education and impose fees. The resulting outcry was well reflected in the hearing of the first Select Committee of 1873 on the Endowed Schools Act. Outraged Conservative opinion is epitomised in the remarks made by Lord Salisbury (again) in the Lords. 'Where the Commissioners found a school in the corner of a county', asserted Salisbury, 'they put it in the middle; where they found a boys' school they turned it into a girls' school'. Quoting these remarks, Lyttleton said that 'what Lord Salisbury meant (for, of course, he could only mean what was literally true)' was not that we had done so, 'but had attempted to do so in one of each such cases'.[12] He mentioned Beaumaris, Wimborne, and Grey Coat schools as the three cases in point. By then, 1873-4, it was evident that the cry 'injustice to the poor' was not only being raised by radical politicians, but also by the Conservative elements in local and national opinion as a means of holding up the Commission's work.

In point of fact, the Commissioners were thwarted by groups called into existence to prevent them doing their work efficiently – especially the Headmasters' Conference, led by Thring, which, in Professor Armytage's words, 'for the last 100 years has acted as the House of Lords in English education, a select, anti-state pressure group'.[13] Collectively, such groups as the Headmasters' Conference and City of London Companies made the Endowed Schools Act and the Commission political hot potatoes, which were consequently dropped by the Tories when they came into power in 1874. The Commission was then abandoned, as is well known, and its powers in educational matters handed to the Charity Commission. But that is another story – another which, incidentally, has not yet been adequately researched.

The Endowed Schools Commissioners may, then, be regarded as a failure. Nevertheless, in reforming Governing Bodies and in the new schemes which they successfully carried through, they did enable the aspiring endowed grammar schools, like Uppingham, Sherborne and Repton, to break their ties with the locality and develop as public schools for a particular social class. In this way they certainly played their part in creating the closed system referred to earlier. But they also played their part, through the new schemes, in *beginning* to rescue the run of the mill local endowed schools from their decrepit state, a function that was carried on by the Charity Commissioners. The fact that they provoked so much opposition that it was found politically rewarding to abolish them may be seen as a tribute to their radicalism (in some respects), and their energy.

Conclusion

In this latter respect, the Endowed Schools Commissioners contrast sharply with the Public Schools and the University Commissioners. Indeed in effect they pursued an opposite policy. The public schools and university Commissioners sought to achieve a consensus with the interests involved, and to soften whatever action they took that might be regarded as radical. In both cases, having achieved their objectives (new governing bodies and statutes) the Commissioners went out of existence, leaving the institutions they had been concerned with to function independently of any state control or even monitoring, yet also in a position to man (sic) the state, both in its political and its bureaucratic aspects. These institutions were now firmly established at the top of the hierarchy. In effect, Parliamentary intervention, taken in both cases at a time when this primacy was threatened, enabled them to adapt themselves to new circumstances, and therefore to retain their traditional supremacy. The lower level institutions with which the Endowed Schools Commissioners were concerned clearly required rather more drastic intervention. Acting as an organ of the state, this is what the Endowed Schools Commissioners tried to achieve. But the necessary consensus to operate precisely in this way was not present in this case. Hence the opposition and final abolition of the Commission – or rather, the transfer of its functions to a more respectable (or accepted) body which, however, continued its work with considerable energy.

From all this we can reasonably conclude that state intervention across the board took, in this period, a decisive form. In the event it operated to firm up and establish a hierarchical structure of education, the base of the pyramid being laid by the passage of the Elementary Education Act of 1870. In effect, it could be argued, this system remained unchanged in its broad outlines for another hundred years or more. For in many respects it is still with us – the only serious dent that has been made is the bringing together of the elementary and secondary school institutions through the development of comprehensive education in the 1960s and 70s, but today even this achievement is under threat.

All this casts some light on the techniques of state intervention, as it has developed historically. Perhaps this analysis, of events taking place more than one hundred years ago, may alert us to take a more sophisticated look at the composition of important committees which chart the future. How are the personnel chosen, why these particular people? What is the role of the officials and, more especially now, the rash of politically appointed quangos who tend to take the place of the Executive Commissioners of the past? What is the relation between the Parliamentary process and educational change? If we have a somewhat ossified educational system in England today, as many think (in spite of the brouhaha occasioned by the 1988 Education Act and subsequent measures), it may be fruitful to seek some, at least, of its origins in the politics of education, and in the different techniques found appropriate at different times to circumvent more democratic processes. It is these which are now again at risk.

Notes

[1] David Ian Allsobrook, *Schools for the Shires: The Reform of Middle-class Education in Mid-Victorian England* (Manchester University Press, 1986); Colin Shrosbree, *Public Schools and Private Education: The Clarendon Commission, 1861-64, and the Public Schools Acts* (Manchester University Press, 1988).

[2] E. Graham, *The Harrow Life of Henry Montagu Butler*, Longmans, 1920, pp207-8.

[3] *Ibid.*, pp208-9.

[4] W.R. Ward, *Victorian Oxford*, (Frank Cass, 1965), p206. Material in the next two paragraphs derives from this source, pp191-2, 209.

[5] *Ibid.*, pp300, 311, 315-6.

[6] In *All Souls in my Time* (Duckworth 1993) the erstwhile radical, A.L. Rowse, for fifty years a fellow, strongly defends the college's existing status and practices.

[7] Hansard, House of Commons, Vol XCXVI, Col 1747, 14 June 1869.

[8] *Report of the Select Committee on the Endowed Schools Act (1868)*, 1873, p18.

[9] Sir Arthur Hobhouse, *The Dead Hand*, London 1880, pp109-10.

[10] *Report of the Endowed Schools Commissioners to Her Majesty's Privy Council*, 1972, p5.

[11] *Ibid.*, pp37-9.

[12] *Report of the Select Committee on the Endowed Schools Act (1868)*, 1873, p80.

[13] W.H.G. Armytage, 'Secondary Education', in Bernard Crick, ed., *Essays in Reform, 1867. A Centenary Tribute* (Oxford 1967).

4: Charity and the 'Public' Schools*

My starting point in ventilating this crucial and delicate issue is this, that we are all victims of legislation carried through in the high Victorian period, for which none of us is responsible. But we have to cope with its outcome. This legislation which related specifically to the uses of charitable support for education, is directly responsible for the fact that even today, as we edge into the twenty-first century, we still do not have a national system of education in this country but a divided one. In this the contrast with our neighbours across the Channel – France and Germany – with the Scandinavian countries, with the United States, Japan, even China and the countries which once comprised the Soviet Union, is striking. I think it is true to say that we are the only advanced industrial country in the world that boasts two systems – one for the wealthier and more privileged, the other for the rest. Indeed until recently, and even today, the schools that were and are considered truly 'national' – the real expression of the national ethos and character – are the public schools, the great bulk of which were established initially through charitable endowments, though as we shall see, these originally took a different form than they do today. There have been efforts to overcome this dichotomy. They have failed. One was made with considerable force during the Second World War, when the public schools faced a fiscal crisis and when their prestige was at a low ebb. Preparation for legislation was made by the Fleming Committee, but this committee took its time and only reported one week before the 1944 Act received Royal Assent. There was, therefore, nothing in the Act on the public schools. 'The first class carriage had been shunted onto an immense siding', as R.A. Butler put

* Invited address to a conference on 'Schools and Charitable Status – New Ways Ahead?' organised by the Directory of Social Change, 20 January 1992.

it in his memoirs in self-congratulation.[1]

The second initiative was the establishment of the Public School Commission by Anthony Crosland in December 1965. This, (the Newsom Commission), reported in April 1968 proposing, incidentally, that all charitable privileges and benefits accorded to the public schools should be abolished. But the report generally did not find general acceptance and the matter was dropped. The government, at that stage, clearly did not have the political will to carry through the 'radical' reform that Crosland himself had called for. Nor did the Commission itself, incidentally, propose such a reform.

So we are left with the current situation, with all its anomalies. And here we are focusing only on one aspect of this – the justification, or otherwise, of the charitable funding which still exists and underpins these schools, and with the various fiscal and other benefits which it brings. The Newsom Commission, which included two public school heads incidentally, clearly thought that there could be no rational justification for these benefits. The purposes of many schools having charitable status, they concluded, seem to be something other than charitable on any ordinary interpretation of the word. It is difficult to see, they added drily, a charitable purpose in relieving parents paying fees of £500 a year or more (today over £5,000). What we have here, they added, is a 'plain anomaly' which has arisen through the complexities of the English law of charities, by which benefits are enjoyed by institutions which are, only in a technical sense, performing a charitable function. The typical public school is after all, they add, an institution providing a service on the basis of parental choice and for substantial fees. It is not easy to defend provisions by which such institutions (and indirectly, their fee-payers) receive, via charitable reliefs, what is in effect a subsidy from the tax payer and the rate payer.[2]

For this reason, that Commission recommended cessation of this practice, as concerns the ordinary public school. They also recommended, incidentally, bringing to an end what are still legal (that is, legitimate) measures to obtain tax relief on school fees which were, and still are, widespread. And here they quote evidence from CASE (Campaign for the Advancement of State Education) on tax rebates available under these schemes:

> Whereas in the public sector all educational expenditure is closely controlled, both nationally and locally, there can be no similar control

exercised by the community over the individual decisions of parents which result in the payment of these rebates. This appears to us to be an indefensible use of public monies when all parts of the state educational system are severely restricted by lack of resources.

This was an important issue, the Commission underlined – a matter for Parliament.[3]

Tax relief and rate relief are the means by which substantial sums of public money are siphoned to the public schools (as 'charities'). The Newsom Commission gave several striking examples of the extent of this funding by the country's tax payers in general. After a thorough investigation, this committee found that pupils were able to attend the most generously endowed schools at a fee much below that which would provide the same services without endowments. In some cases the value of these endowments is now enormous (BS). Twenty years ago the Commission found that, of about one hundred schools answering their enquiries, six had an income from these sources amounting to more than 25% of their total income, two between 20% and 25%, twenty-two between 10% and 20%, and fifty-six between 5% and 10%. At the most generously endowed boys schools, they said, the probability was that the annual fees might be 20 per cent higher on average if it were not for income from sources other than fees. It is right, the Commission concluded, that parents should be free to pay school fees if they wish; but, not right that they should, without good reason, be relieved by the Exchequer or local authorities of part of the true cost of what they are buying. 'At the very least', the Commission comments, 'the public should be aware of the contribution it is making'.[4]

I want to suggest that we need to understand something of the historical origins of all this, if we are to form a clear view. Endowments to support education have a long history in this country. These covered all levels of education but by the early nineteenth century their administration was subject to much criticism due to corruption, inefficiency, mismanagement and the longueurs of the Court of Chancery, which was supposed to set things right. The passage of the Education Act of 1870, however, created a new situation as far as endowments for elementary education were concerned. The Act was intended to provide education out of rates and taxes. What, then, should happen to these endowments?

The answer seemed simple to the Victorians. Middle-class education was in a mess and required resources. The working class was now provided for by the Elementary Education Act. The resources, in the form of these ancient endowments should, then, be transferred to the middle classes and used to support fee-paying systems of education for them. In Loughborough, for instance – an area I have studied – the whole complex of schools for the people of the town, based on earlier endowments and covering all levels of education, was broken up, the bulk of the endowments constituting the Town Estate, and under local control, went to support two middle-class schools (one for boys, one for girls), now no longer under the control of the local inhabitants. This was not achieved, of course, without massive local protests. But it was in fact carried through quite ruthlessly.[5] These two schools incidentally, are now independent, the boys' school a member of the Headmasters Conference, so rating as a 'public' school.

This kind of thing went on all over the country. A crucial role in this restructuring, and transfer of endowments, was played by the Endowed Schools Commission appointed following the report of the Schools Inquiry Commission and the 1869 Endowed Schools Act. The Schools Inquiry Commission held that it should be possible, by utilising existing endowments and re-organising them on a rational basis, to establish a complete, modernised and effective system of education for the middle classes, both boys and girls. This policy failed, as was recognised by the Bryce Commission on secondary education thirty years later. Hence the belated intervention by the state in 1902. But the Endowed Schools Commission, appointed under the Act of 1869, set about attempting to achieve this with some energy. A major objective was to abolish free education, as laid down in many grammar and local school statutes; to take over the endowments and use them to fund specifically middle-class schools at three levels, Grades 1, 2 and 3 – tailored to meet the needs of the upper middle class, the middle middle class and the lower middle class, in the words of the Commission's report. The higher the grade of school being established, the greater the resources required, as the Commission itself had argued in its report: 'An application of endowments becomes increasingly needful as the education becomes higher' – so the Grade 1 schools, for the upper middle class, were to get most of the money.[6]

The money itself was obtained partly by the total, and ruthless abolition of the rights to a free education which obtained in many localities, and indeed had been insisted on by the donors and inscribed in the statutes of many endowed schools. The Schools Inquiry Commission thoroughly disapproved of what they termed 'indiscriminate gratuitous instruction'. This was a waste of endowments, they claimed, 'as invariably mischievous as indiscriminate alms giving', and should be abolished.[7] Instead of free education, fees should be charged, and exhibitions provided for a small proportion open to public competition. This is the origin of the scholarships, bursaries, etc, available at many public schools today – they represent, in attenuated form, the ancient rights to a free education for local populations insisted on by the founders.

All over the country, similar transformations were brought about as at Loughborough – at Bedford, for instance, where there was, and is, a large and wealthy endowment, the Commissioners proposed that, 'after the lapse of a certain number of years, the exclusive privilege of the town of Bedford should cease'. We should then, they continued triumphantly, 'have an educational endowment of £10,000 a year to be made the most of, freed from local restrictions as to those who are to benefit from it'.[8] So a new school 'for the extension of middle-class education' could be largely financed from an endowment intended to provide free education for the people of Bedford.

As this policy was put into practice by the Endowed Schools commissioners in the early 1870s, protests broke out in villages, market towns and elsewhere all over the country. At Scarning in Norfolk, at Kendal further north, at Sutton Coldfield in the Midlands, the removal of the traditional rights to a free education met a massive and in some cases an implacable opposition – often from local working men and women and local communities generally. At Sutton Coldfield, where elementary education had been free through endowments, £15,000 was now appropriated to build a grammar school – described in a Parliamentary inquiry as 'a high school for well to do children'; it was also proposed to appropriate a further £17,000 to build and endow a high school for girls. In Kendal, thousands signed protests against a scheme to appropriate resources providing free education in a local Blue Coat school to develop boarding facilities for the well to do in the local grammar school. A public meeting in 1884 reflected 'very great feeling on the subject', and approved a report which concluded:

The interference by the Commissioners, here and in many other places, has aroused the people to action in defence of their rights, which can be maintained by united action and by using every constitutional means, which in the end cannot fail to receive justice.

Their hope was not to be realised.[9] The result here and elsewhere was that, by the 1890s, the middle classes of the country enjoyed a subsidised system of secondary education; one established largely at the expense of the working class.

But the biggest privatisation, and this is what it was, of public resources – that carried through on the most massive scale – was the privatisation of Eton College and its assets; the leading public school, but one which, through a mixture of corruption and stagnation, had to be reformed in the mid-nineteenth century if it was to survive and continue to play its crucial role in the social and political circumstances of this country. This process, which relates to the Clarendon Commission and the establishment of the category of public schools as a separate legal category, has recently been acutely studied by Colin Shrosbree in his scholarly analysis entitled *The Public Schools and Private Education: The Clarendon Commission 1861-64 and the Public Schools Act*,[10] published by Manchester University Press in 1988. Shrosbree has thrown a flood of new light on this whole area. The story he tells is extraordinary.

What emerges is that there was, at this time, (the late 1860s), the clear determination to carry through Parliament an essentially conservative measure having the purpose of creating what Shrosbree calls 'a new kind of school, with Eton as its model, founded on public funds but available only through fees'. Fearful of the effect of the extension of the franchise in 1867, Shrosbree sees the Public Schools Act of 1868 as 'a pre-emptive claim to Eton and the other great schools – a defence of political and educational advantage in the face of imminent democracy.'[11]

When this Act was under discussion in Parliament, special care was taken to confine discussion and debate, so far as possible, to the Lords. This ensured that the few radical MPs now represented in the Commons would be effectively excluded. When the Bill did eventually reach the Commons there was little opportunity for serious amendment. The Public Schools Act, Shrosbree concludes, 'became an effective means of transferring public endowments, and the great educational assets of buildings and historic sites, from the community to private use.'[12]

We must remember that this transfer of public endowments not only underpinned the restructuring and establishment of the leading seven (or nine) 'Great' schools, not only Eton, but Rugby, Harrow and others as well, but also, through the parallel Endowed Schools Act, the mass of the now restructured endowed schools for the middle classes, for instance, Loughborough, Oundle, Repton and many others. On this whole exercise I would like to quote Shrosbree's own conclusions:

> Public assets and public funding are adapted to serve private interests. Public assets are bought or monopolised by those who can afford to pay. Public services are both impoverished and placed in competition with private agencies which do not have the burdens of public responsibility, even though they may benefit from considerable public subsidy. Public subsidy is not only divorced from public responsibility but used to fund the pursuit of private interest and social inequality ... The history of secondary education in England since the Public Schools Acts must raise doubts about whether free, public, democratic education can survive erosion by class attitudes, financial inequalities and the neglect of public services in favour of private interest.[13]

Now let me address the question we were asked to discuss:

'Schools that already have more than others – can they justify their use of charitable funding?'
My answer is No. What we have here is probably the biggest hijack of public resources, its direction to private purposes, in history. That operation was spread over roughly half a century, but finally successfully carried through by an unreformed Parliament representative of the aristocracy and landed interest in particular, fearful of the imminent extension of democracy which, as foreseen, was bound to put the public interest before the private.

No one knows, or has calculated, so far as I know, the extent of the hijack (or the booty). A typical well-heeled public school gives the insurance value of its properties as nearly £80 million at 1989 values.[14] Some of this may not represent endowment assets, but be the result of gifts and appeals later; but if there were thirty schools at this level, that gives a total of £2,400,000,000, or nearly £2½ billion. That is quite a sum. These resources attract tax relief on their income. The accounts of the school I've mentioned show that, in 1989, the school had a shortfall of about £200,000 on its expenditure – that is, the fees income was short of expenditure by that amount. What happens? An equivalent sum, indeed much more, is transferred from the Trust income to make up the difference. That sum is tax free, and therefore includes a substantial public subsidy. That, I suggest, is morally unacceptable – totally.

But there is a bigger problem, raised by this whole issue. Should there not be an Act of Restitution? Our Prime Minister stands for a classless society – or so he tells us. The fact that he sends his own son to a public school hardly gives confidence in the reality of this objective. A more convincing action would be a clear determination to tackle this whole issue, which relates not only to the question of charity but more importantly to that of the construction of a truly national system of education. To achieve this, the Victorian legislation needs to be undone, lock, stock and barrel. This is a matter for Parliament.

Father Dominic Milroy, head of Ampleforth and the new Chairman of the Headmasters Conference, is reported as concluding his first address as chairman recently with these words:[15]

> We have been challenged to justify the charitable status of our schools, rather than to take it for granted, and this is a challenge which most of us would regard as perfectly fair.

I have attempted to do just this, and no more. But such a challenge as I hope I have made raises some very deep social, educational and historical issues which, I suggest, we need to face squarely. If we are all prepared to recognise the injustices that have been done, then we will have found the common ground which we must find, if an acceptable, forward-looking and above all equitable solution is to be found.

Notes

[1] Lord Butler, *The Art of the Possible* (London, 1971), p120.
[2] Public School Commission, First Report, Vol 1, *Report*, HMSO, 1968, pp157-63.
[3] *Ibid.*, p161.
[4] *Ibid.*, pp158-60.
[5] Brian Simon, ed., *Education in Leicestershire, 1540-1940*, (Leicester, 1968), p154.
[6] Report of Schools Inquiry Commission, 1868, Vol 1, p167.
[7] *Ibid.*, Vol 1, pp593-94.
[8] *Ibid.*, Vol 1, pp534-35.
[9] See Brian Simon, *The Two Nations and the Educational Structure, 1780-1870*, (London, 1960), pp329-33.
[10] Colin Shrosbree, *The Public Schools and Private Education: The Clarendon Commission 1861-64 and the Public Schools Acts*, (Manchester, 1988).
[11] *Ibid.*, p177.
[12] *Ibid.*, p221.
[13] *Ibid*, p222-23.

[14] The Governing Body of Rugby School: Report and Financial Statement for the Year Ended 31st August 1989. (Source: Charity Commission Registry).
[15] *Education*, 17 January 1992.

5: Education and Citizenship in England*

I would like to start with a quotation – very familiar to me, since it was framed like a picture and hung on my nursery wall. It remained there through my early youth. It was circulated as a Christmas card by my father, just elected Lord Mayor of Manchester, in 1921 – just three years after World War One, in which he lost his three brothers. It is a quotation from Pericles' famous speech (or funeral oration) commemorating the men who died during the decisive victory at the Battle of Salamis. 'Such then is the city for whom, lest they should lose her, the men who we celebrate died a soldier's death. And it is but natural that all of us, who survive them, should wish to spend ourselves in her service.'

'To spend ourselves in her service.' Such, then, was the ideal of citizenship – of the role of the free citizen in a democratic society (or state). But, of course, this freedom, and the opportunity to fulfill this function, was procured (in the Greek city-state) at the expense of an underclass; the slaves, who in their turn were denied any participation as citizens of the state. So there you have what was certainly a noble ideal, but with a canker at its heart.

As far as my country is concerned, these ideals are no more easily combined than they were in Ancient Greece. Ambiguities in the political idea of citizenship were, in many countries, accompanied by similar ambiguities in the field of education. Does the lasting gap between the 'public' school and popular education in England merely

* Delivered at a conference on 'Quality of Citizenship' at the University of Utrecht in March 1991.

imply that equal citizenship is still incomplete? Or is it principally impossible to conceive of citizenship without taking into account those frictions and tensions?

England is a country which formed its educational concepts primarily for elites. The concept of the 'gentleman' is a prototype of an imperfect citizenship. He must and can only be the product of a specific, segregated education – of which the ideal type is now and for long has been a member of the landed gentry or aristocracy educated at Eton and Christ Church College, Oxford (or Trinity College, Cambridge). This essentially exclusive education having, as an inevitable by-product, its own specific culture and ethos whose value derives specifically from the fact that such an education is not, by definition, available to the broad masses – nor even to more than a tiny minority of the nascent middle class in all its varied sub-divisions. The 'gentleman' – the product of a close relation between both education (on the one hand) and up-bringing (on the other) is specifically recognizable (or defined) in the sense that his speech (and use of language), his deportment and behaviour generally, differs from that of all other members of society. So, although all might, in a formal sense, be citizens of one society; that common experience is and was rent by 'frictions and tensions'. The educational system of England (and I am confining myself deliberately to England rather than Great Britain), it can and has been argued by many authorities, far from being designed to encourage common experiences and a common culture, has operated to enhance, and even to exacerbate, already existing social differences and experiences. Far from a solvent, it became a separator, a means by which differences may be, and are perpetuated.

The ironic feature here is that, as the formal rights of citizenship were extended, particularly through successive extensions of the franchise (the right to vote for members of Parliament), so, coincidentally, systems (and later complex sub-systems) of education, now covering the entire population, were constructed which, in the minds of their architects, deliberately aimed at accentuating social, or class, differences. What was given with one hand (often as a direct result of mass, popular pressure in the form of continuous demonstrations and, at certain times, even the threat of revolution) was taken away with the other. It is this (latter) process which is worth analysis.

In the great re-organisation (but scarcely modernisation) of English education that took place between the years 1850 and 1870, no less than five Royal Commissions investigated all levels of schooling and the universities and made their recommendations. Each was followed by Acts of Parliament. The basic principle of re-organisation that emerged was that education must be restructured on lines of social class. Indeed this was specifically stated by the most important of these commissions, the Schools Inquiry Commission (or Taunton Commission), in its report of 1868 as we have already seen (Chapter 2, p28).

What emerged was a system comprising as many as five sub-systems, or levels:

First, the public schools (Eton, Harrow, etc.) for the aristocracy, gentry, and the professional classes related to these (clergy, army and navy, legal profession, perhaps banking).
Second, three grades or levels of 'grammar' or 'endowed' schools:
Grade 1: for the upper-middle class.
Grade 2: for what the Schools Enquiry Commission defined as the 'middle-middle' class.
Grade 3: for the lower-middle class.
Third, (or fifth), the 'elementary' schools for the working class (established universally as a sub-system in the decade 1870-1880).

And what was the political, or social function of popular education as seen at that time (late 1860s)? Here we can do no better than move to Robert Lowe, leading British statesman, who totally opposed the extension of the franchise in 1867 and, defeated in that, launched his 'education campaign' which embodied also its reform. In his view, education was the key to the future – it was 'a question of self-preservation ... a question of existence, even of the existence of our Constitution'.[1] Both upper-class and lower-class education needed reform.

If the lower classes, he wrote, must now be educated 'to qualify them for the power that has passed ... into their hands', the higher classes must be educated differently because power has passed out of their hands – in short, they must preserve their position by 'superior education and superior cultivation'. Above all, this education must be up-to-date so that they 'know the things the working men know, only know them infinitely better in their principles and in their details': thereby they can 'assert their superiority' over the workers, a superiority ensured by 'greater intelligence and leisure', and so 'conquer back by means of a wider and more enlightened cultivation some of the influence they have lost by political change'.[2]

Lowe is quite clear that political considerations must dictate educational change, and equally clear about the political objectives educational reform is to serve. If the lower classes must now be educated to discharge their new duties, they must also 'be educated that they may appreciate and defer to a higher cultivation when they meet it; and the higher classes', Lowe goes on, 'ought to be educated in a very different manner, in order that they may exhibit to the lower classes that higher education to which, if it were shown to them, they would bow down and defer'.[3]

What concept of citizenship is it, that is founded on the precept that the great mass of the people, to be educated in elementary schools, must be so inducted as to 'bow down and defer' to an elite group, having quite other educational experiences, the product of which is 'superior cultivation'?

It is an historical fact – or series of facts – that educational transformation in England has, over the last 160 years or more, been very closely related to the slow reform and extension of the franchise. The right to vote – to have a direct say in the election of representatives to Parliament, and so on legislation – must surely be rated as an essential element in any true citizenship. But from the first there was a fear that, if the franchise was extended to the mass of the people (male and female), they would exercise their rights, and send their own representatives to Parliament who would legislate in their own interests, and so certainly transform the existing social order.

Such fears were widespread in the early nineteenth century, when, due to mounting opposition to the corrupt, irrational and highly restrictive (or exclusive) nature of the existing franchise system, parliamentary reform, long demanded, was becoming a political necessity.

It was the ideologists, and political representatives, of the emergent industrial middle class, who now saw their opportunity. How to break the power of the semi-feudal aristocracy and gentry who had governed England for so long, but whose legislative powers, in both Houses of Parliament (Lords *and* Commons) were used to obstruct the free development and exploitation of capital? Extend the franchise, bring in not only the middle class in the new urban conglomerations in the North of England, but also, and more specifically, the now growing and greatly more numerous working class. With a reformed franchise, these together would have the power to do the job.

But ... and it was a big but: the enfranchisement of the people (conferring on them the most basic right and symbol of citizenship) must be accompanied, it was argued (for instance, and especially, by Jeremy Bentham and James Mill) by a vast expansion of popular education, the object of which should be, to teach the people where their true interests lay. And, according to these publicists, their interest lay, not in attacking the free play of capital, and capitalist development, but in supporting it. The true interests of both capitalist and worker, they argued, were one and the same: to break the barriers which obstructed the free play of capital, the essential preliminary of which was to oust the representatives of the landed interest from the monopoly of political power.

Hence the widespread educational, and political, campaign carried through by the Utilitarians (sometimes called Philosophic Radicals) in the late 1820s and early 1830s both for the extension of the franchise to all males over twenty-one (or, in the case of Bentham, both males *and* females), and for the provision of popular education on a massive scale, having this specific aim and content.[4] This latter initiative, incidentally, received the full support of the classical political economists, Ricardo and Malthus – both following in the footsteps of Adam Smith, who also saw education as a 'public good', if largely as a potent, and necessary, means of social control.[5]

Forty years later it was the further extension of the franchise (in 1867) that lay behind Robert Lowe's educational 'campaign', having the content, and the objectives, already described. In the meantime, the systematic stratification of English education ensured that the conditions now existed whereby each social class (and even fractions of social classes) received a specific, differentiated education, considered appropriate to the social role and status of each.

As noted elsewhere (Chapter 2, p28), nineteenth century historians, for instance Best and Perkin, are generally agreed that the restructuring of education during this century re-inforced, and indeed exacerbated class differences.[6]

This analysis (or thesis), originally made many years ago, has recently received further support from two scholarly studies, both recently published as books, but both originally doctoral dissertations. One of them is concerned with the elite public schools, and specifically with the Royal Commission that examined these (the Clarendon Commission, which reported in 1864), the other with the more general endowed (or usually 'grammar') schools – the Schools Enquiry (or Taunton) Commission, reporting in 1868.

Public Schools and Private Education, by Colin Shrosbree (1988), is a detailed, specialist analysis of the Clarendon Commission and subsequent legislation. Shrosbree shows beyond any question that this Commission, which was set up in 1861, operated, in fact, as a front for a whole series of highly questionable manoeuvres directed specifically at salvaging (and actually privatising) Eton College, then and now the leading school for the governing class or groups in Britain from going down under the weight of outraged criticism at the malpractices then existing. To salvage this particular school – given its social role historically – was then seen, by the elite groups, as essential. For here was the ideal type education conferring specific distinction to the concept, and realisation, of the 'gentleman'.[7]

In *Schools for the Sixties* (1986) David Allsobrook has made a parallel, and again very specific analysis of the work of the crucial Schools Inquiry Commission, whose brief was to examine, and report on, all schools lying between the so-called 'public' schools on the one hand, and the elementary schools, examined by the Newcastle Commission in the late 1850s on the other. These were the 800 odd endowed (grammar) schools, largely founded in the sixteenth and seventeenth centuries. Allsobrook's research shows, beyond any reasonable doubt (and this is a novel interpretation), that the work and recommendations of this Commission, and the legislation that followed its report, must be seen as representing the victory of the aristocratic-gentry element in mid-Victorian society, and certainly not that of the rising bourgeoisie, or capitalist middle class.[8] So, as I suggested at the start, the restructuring of English education, the grounds for which were laid in the two decades 1850-1870, can hardly be assessed as a modernising process (except, perhaps, insofar as they led to a full systematisation of this structure) – nor as a means of enhancing a participant citizenship. Rather this process was directed, and deliberately so, to enhancement of social differences and so the perpetuation of the status quo in which the products of one sub-division (public schools), with the help of those of another (Grade 1 endowed schools), governed and controlled the products of all the others. In spite of modifications over the past century, the structure of this system has remained basically unchanged.

Is it partly the result of this situation that a vibrant socially responsible citizenship, or concept of this, hardly exists today in England – indeed recently, from the highest level, the very concept of the existence of a society of which the individual is part, and which he or she might serve (in the Periclean sense) has been called into question

– even denied. 'There is no such thing as society', Margaret Thatcher was reported as saying in the late 1980s, 'only individuals'.

In contradistinction to this thinking, perhaps specifically (or deliberately), there is today a new initiative afoot – having cross party support, and that of the Speaker of the House of Commons. This move, coming 'from above' (as it were), is concerned with the deliberate attempt to 'teach' citizenship through the schools and educational system generally.[9]

This is not, by any means, the first such initiative. In the late 1930s an Association for Education in Citizenship was established, also having prestigious, all-party support. It aimed to provide a counter to the contemporary appeal of fascism (in Germany) and to communism (in Russia) – a sort of democratic alternative. This organisation was ambitious. It aimed to transform teaching in all subjects – mathematics, science, as well as history, geography, English, and so on, in all schools both elementary and secondary (including teacher training) so that they all introduced 'citizenship' issues as central, right across the board. This was a voluntary organisation, and, since in England then the state did not intervene in the curriculum, could hope for success. It was, in fact, a truly 'liberal' initiative; as a matter of fact the initiative was taken, and most of the organising work done, by my father E.D. Simon.[10] This initiative was, however, overtaken by the Second World War and made no lasting impression.

To turn to the current initiative, mentioned earlier – this is now under way. It may have a greater hope of success because, since the 1988 Education Act, the state now controls programmes of study in all the main subjects in the schools, so decisions taken centrally can now affect what is taught in all schools between the ages of five and sixteen (except, significantly, in independent schools which are exempt). But, in spite of this move, there is at present little sign of any encouragement towards the creation of an ethos of active citizenship among the people generally. Even existing forms and structures which, potentially, might allow such developments – I refer to local government and the local franchise – are now, as a result of a series of hammer blows over the last decade, very seriously at risk. The reasons for the current attack by central on local government are both financial and directly political.

If the main function of education is to operate to perpetuate, or exacerbate, existing social (or class) differences, as I believe historically has been the case in England, then its total effect must be inimical to the interests of the country as a whole. Further, by erecting what are generally (for the mass of the people) insurmountable obstacles, it is a force denying the possibility of a true and active citizenship for all. In these circumstances, actually to teach 'citizenship' in the schools may be no more than a new means of habituating the population to the political (or social) system as it actually now exists. But this, as we have seen, has always been a major function of education in England, both as concerns its structure and its content.

A true teaching of citizenship today, which aims actually to achieve it as a reality, must involve critical analysis, and must aim at transformation – both of education and of the social order. But how can this be achieved within an educational system whose social role is seen, by those in authority, as the preservation of that order? Or is this a special problem for those of us who live across the Channel?

That is the question that I would like to leave with you.

Notes

1 Robert Lowe, *Primary and Classical Education* (London, 1867), I, pp8-10.

2 *Ibid.*, pp31-32.

3 *Ibid.*, p32. Lowe became Chancellor of the Exchequer in the Gladstone administration formed in 1868; he was, therefore, in a good position to influence the character and passage of the 1870 Education Act.

4 The thesis (of the 'democratic model') given in the last few paragraphs is presented in greater detail in Brian Simon, *Studies in the History of Education, 1780-1870* (London, 1960), retitled *The Two Nations and the Educational Structure, 1780-1870* (London, 1974), especially in chapter 2, 'Education and the Struggle for Reform, 1800-1832', and chapter 7, 'The State and Education (3) Elementary Schooling for the Working Class'. It is developed in Brian Simon, *Education and the Labour Movement, 1870-1920* (London, 1965).

5 Simon, *The Two Nations*, pp138-43.

6 Harold Perkin, *The Origins of Modern British Society, 1790-1880* (London, 1959), p302; Geoffrey Best, *Mid-Victorian Britain 1851-1875* (London, 1973), p170.

7 Colin Shrosbree, *Public Schools and Private Education. The Clarendon Commission 1861-1864 and the Public Schools Acts* (Manchester, 1988).

8 David Ian Allsobrook, *Schools for the Shires. The Reform of Middle Class Education in Mid-Victorian England* (Manchester, 1986).

9 National Curriculum Council, *Education for Citizenship* (London, 1990).

10 See Sir Ernest Simon and Eva M. Hubback, *Training for Citizenship* (Oxford, 1935). This sets out the general objectives of this movement. See also Association for Education in Citizenship, *Education for Citizenship in Secondary Schools* (Oxford, 1936), with Foreword by Oliver Stanley, President of the Board of Education, and *Education for Citizenship in Elementary*

Schools (Oxford, 1939), with Foreword by the Rt. Hon the Earl Baldwin of Bewdley KG.

6: The Universities and Social Change*

The struggle to broaden access to our universities, of which the foundation of the University of Lancaster is a part, has a long history, often forgotten. It is now 350 years since the 'Nobility, Gentry, Clergy, Freeholders and other Inhabitants of the Northern parts of England' (as they described themselves) submitted a petition to Lord Fairfax, maintaining that the lack of a University in northern England was 'a great prejudice to the Kingdom in general, but a greater misery and unhappiness to these countries in particular, many ripe and hopeful wits being utterly lost for want of education'.[1] The petition failed. Parliament, Fairfax advised, was too busy on more critical matters to give serious consideration to the proposal. It is true that a university was started at Durham shortly after, but it did not survive. The ripe and hopeful wits from this part of the country continued, therefore, to be utterly lost for want of education until shall we say (since this is a celebratory occasion) 1962, when Lancaster university was effectively established. The petitioners' proposal, incidentally, had been for a university at Manchester, and not at Lancaster in spite of its proximity to the Cumberland schools which were later to flourish. Cumberland and North Lancastrian youth would for many centuries have to take the road to Cambridge (more usually than Oxford) and, on the journey home, be overwhelmed by the first view of Windermere from Orrest Head, as William Wordsworth was on his return from his first year at Cambridge.[2]

Effectively to extend access to higher education was, of course a major objective for Charles Carter, whose endeavours in this and related fields this series of lectures specifically celebrates. Discussing this question in his recent publication *Our Age*, Noel Annan, himself a distinguished ex-Vice Chancellor, bemoans our failure effectively to

* The Charles Carter (annual) lecture, delivered at the University of Lancaster, 20 November 1990.

84

extend access, especially across the binary divide. 'Only Charles Carter', he says, 'one of the few Vice Chancellors with imagination about the future (and therefore regarded by right-minded professors as a dangerous man), envisaged a civic university as a planet with satellite colleges exchanging students'.[3] This, from such a source, is certainly an accolade. By these actions, I understand, the net has been cast wider here in a determined effort to recover some, at least, of the ripe and hopeful wits whose exclusion was already deplored several centuries ago.

The pressure to extend access to higher education is, then, no new-fangled modern concern. It has a long history, as have other attempts to transform existing procedures. In the late 1930s, for instance, to cite just one example with which I'm familiar, many students began to feel strongly that, as students, they were excluded from any say whatever in the government and direction of the universities they attended. There was then a movement, shared by some staff, increasingly critical both of the content of education as transmitted (or 'delivered' as the jargon now goes), and of the manner by which this was done. 'Reform it altogether', we used to say, following Hamlet – but how? Inquiries were undertaken, reports produced – even joint staff-student meetings held. But did these have any effect? Kind words were spoken, since the students of that generation did not see the universities as arms of a hostile state, meet to be overthrown. On the contrary, all they asked for was their transformation.

In this situation, I remember, inspiration was derived from delving into Hastings Rashdall's great historical work on mediaeval universities, then recently re-issued in a modern, revised edition. There we discovered the existence of the great student-controlled universities such as Bologna, still one of Italy's leading universities. There it was the students who established the university, hired and paid the teachers, told them what and even how to teach – the professor, for instance, had to reach a definite point in the text by a certain date (a rule which became universal in the law universities of Southern Europe); he was fined if he skipped a chapter, and expressly forbidden to postpone a difficulty to the end of the lecture. At Bologna it was the students who directed the university, elected the Rector, determined the conditions of service, how much the professors should be paid, what holidays they should have. It was the students who handed out leave passes if the lecturer wished to depart for whatever reason for a few days. Professors had to swear obedience to the students' rector, and to obey any other regulations which the university might think fit to impose on them.[4] One wonders if those who now advocate that universities should be financed by full fee payments by the students have really thought through the full implications of their proposals.

An echo of this tradition is still, of course, to be found north of the border, where the student body of the different universities still have the right to elect the Rector who acts as Chair of the Governing Body (or Council) of the university – a right now in danger of abolition by our 'reforming' government. All this was grist to the mill of the 1930s students. In a charter of student rights and responsibilities drawn up exactly fifty years ago – in 1940 – the National Union of Students demanded representation on Senate and Council as well as on Faculty Boards.[5] Perhaps it was the traditional inertia of universities that meant that, following the war, no action whatever was taken on these issues, one result being, perhaps, the student upsurge of the late 1960s when a new generation began now to insist on implementation. So, although the time span is long, change does happen, even within these august institutions.

But does it? Or are such changes merely illusory? A means of adapting existing power relations to new circumstances? The received view among sociologists recently, as I understand it, is that a basic social function of universities, in the Western world at least, is to ensure perpetuation of the existing social order. The leading French sociologist, Pierre Bourdieu, in particular presents this view, arguing the thesis that educational systems, and particularly the institutions at their apex (the universities), generally ensure, through utilisation of a whole number of subtle, unacknowledged and unrecognised procedures, almost precise reproduction of the existing social order. He prefaces his penetrating book on the topic (entitled *Reproduction in Education, Society and Culture*) with a short satirical poem by Robert Desnos (*Chantefleurs, Chantefables*):[6]

> Le capitaine Jonathan,
> Etant âgé de dix-huit ans,
> Capture un jour un pélican
> Dans une île d'Extrême Orient.
> Le pélican de Jonathan,
> Au matin, pond un oeuf tout blanc
> Et il en sort un pélican
> Lui ressemblant étonnamment,
> Et ce deuxième pélican
> Pond, à son tour, un oeuf tout blanc

D'où sort, inévitablement,
Un autre qui en fait autant.
Cela peut durer trés longtemps
Si l'òn ne fait pas d'omelette avant.

The main means, according to Bourdieu, by which what we may call established social classes protect and perpetuate their social status is by the accumulation of what he terms 'cultural capital'. This applies particularly to the academic world, and also to sections of the professional classes generally, particularly those allied to church and state (characterised by Gramsci as 'organic intellectuals'). The easiest way to illustrate this is, perhaps, through an example – of what may be termed an 'ideal type' of such reproduction. I will eschew Noel Annan's masterly study of the intellectual aristocracy and their family connections, though the cases cited there are, of course, closely relevant.[7] Indeed I will start with a single case, which presents a striking example of this process – that of the Temple family.

Octavius Temple, army officer, married in 1805, fathered fifteen children before he died in 1834, eight of whom 'grew up'. Frederick was the thirteenth. His wife, fairly impecunious as a widow, taught all her children to read and write, elementary arithmetic (though she couldn't do it herself), Latin (at twelve, Frederick went to school 'knowing his grammar perfectly'), and Euclid. Octavius managed to get his two younger sons, Frederick and John, a cheap education at a local grammar school (Blundell's school). Of the two, it was Frederick who was the more successful. When at Balliol, to which he won a Scholarship, he consistently rose at 4.30 am, started work at 5.00 am and continued till 3.00 pm, doing what he called his 'easy work' in the evening. Frederick accordingly gained a double first in classics and mathematics. He became head of Rugby, Bishop of Exeter then of London, and finally in 1896, Archbishop of Canterbury. He wrote the crucial chapters – it is said in two days – of the Schools Inquiry Commission's report which aimed to reorganise ancient endowments to create a stratified system of secondary education for the likes of his family.[8]

One of Frederick's sons was William Temple. He in his turn gained a Major Leaving Exhibition to Balliol when at Rugby. Although his biographer (Iremonger) says his papers for this examination 'displayed the worst scholarship work the college had ever decorated, he was elected (on promise rather than performance) to an exhibition, and thereafter did exactly what was required and expected of him'.[9] He, in his turn, became Head of Repton (1910), Bishop of Manchester (1920), Archbishop of York (1929) and finally also Archbishop of Canterbury (1942). So, from a relatively impecunious family there emanated two Archbishops of Canterbury – father and son. No one made an omelette of them.

One thing is clear. To obtain maximum benefit, financial and otherwise, from the system required intense effort, strict planning and often energetic support from a family. A striking example of what was entailed is provided by Robert Skidelsky in his biography of Maynard Keynes. His father, Neville, was the son of a self-made businessman who attributed his success to hard work and religious principles. Neville himself did a ten-hour day at University College, London, gaining a first, but thereafter his academic career misfired, Neville abandoning scholarly endeavours and ending up as a leading official at Cambridge, but determined that his children should make good. Throughout Maynard's early life, Neville planned and supervised every aspect of his son's studies – especially when he entered him for the Eton College scholarship examination. Neville was determined to leave nothing to chance. Special tutors were engaged. Father and son started getting up at 7.00 a.m. every morning and working together before breakfast to accustom Maynard to the times of the scholarship papers. By the time he, his wife Florence and Maynard left for Eton he was, as he put it in his diary, 'in a fearful state of worry'. To make matters worse their hotel in the High Street was 'frightfully noisy', so that he lay awake all night with his gloomy thoughts. After they had returned home Neville continued to worry about the results; but a telegram came. He had pulled through. 'Maynard 10th College Scholar'. This, he wrote, was 'the most delightful telegram I ever received'.

Eight years later the same tactics were employed for the tripos examination at Cambridge. Here again it was his father, Neville, who planned every aspect of the revision, of course with Maynard's co-operation. When the exam was on, Neville, who lived nearby, rose early every morning, walked to King's College, woke Maynard up and set him to work. One day he found Maynard in his bath twenty-five minutes before the exam was due to start; but at last, all was over. 'Maynard has judged his final sprint to perfection', he wrote in his diary. He came out 12th Wrangler. But maths was not to be his subject. A few days later he started work on Marshall's *Principles of Economics*.[10]

This rigorous, indeed almost pathological concern clearly resulted in success – and the perpetuation of this particular pelican, though May-nard did not (so far as is known) initiate the next cycle by producing his own pelican egg. No omelette had to be made in this case to bring the process to a halt – and this minor demographic fact does disrupt proceedings – of course. But case histories of this kind, which could certainly be multiplied, illustrate the Bourdieu thesis. The unity of the language, culture, morality, ethos of the home and of the schools and universities that served these families enabled those with cultural capital to maximise their gains from the educative experience, quite apart from the links and networks that now became available to them. But what chance would a miner's son (or, for that matter, daughter) from Cumbria, say, have had in any similar racecourse? So the procedures securing perpetuation of established social hierarchies remain in place – is it surprising that to breach them requires almost superhuman energy – or great good luck? Yes, it sometimes happens, but it is scarcely usual. Procedures, of course, have changed – but objectively they provide the same obstacles as the more arcane customs of the past. The patterns I've described are part of the warp and woof of British (or more accurately English) social history – deeply engrained in the nature, or culture, of our society, as of others as well. Their roots lie deep.

This is why universities everywhere have been extremely resistant to any attempt radically to alter their social composition – even those that wish to do so. In this country, in spite of the attempt, often heroic, to widen access through the provision of specific courses, even on a large scale and quite deliberately, sociological researches have indicated no serious shift in the composition of the student body over the years. This is not only the experience here, it is that of other countries as well. A most striking case, for instance, is the relative failure of the very deliberate attempts by the Bolsheviks to transform the intake of Moscow University and other institutions of higher education in the years following the 1917 revolution. This is detailed in Sheila Fitzpatrick's study on the issue.[11] Moscow is, of course, the leading (élite) university in Russia, equivalent in status, say, to the University of Tokyo in Japan, the Sorbonne in France and, I suppose, Oxford and Cambridge here. To bring representatives of new social classes into the university there proved to be a far harder task than had been imagined. Krushchev, you will remember, was a product of an access course (known as a *Rabfak* – a workers' faculty); but, so far as I know, never penetrated Moscow University. It was the representatives of those with cultural capital who tended to predominate, even after what was, perhaps, the most striking social and political upheaval in history.

The thesis advanced by Pierre Bourdieu and, as we shall see, other social scientists, appears then accurately to reflect what actually happens; that the universities have operated, as it were inevitably (if in a covert, though certainly not conspiratorial manner) to reproduce society with all its gradations – or, if not quite this, to reinforce the hegemony of established social classes, and to act therefore as a barrier to others. How, then, could it be even conceivably possible that universities might be the agents of social change? How could they operate to break a structure which, it is argued, and with some truth, increasingly hardened with the passage of the centuries – to break the pelican's egg and make an omelette? Surely their role must be the precise opposite.

But the trouble with this analysis – or, shall we say, with this particular standpoint – is that it is unable to encompass the evident actual experience of the coincidence of social and institutional change – or to provide tools that could account for it. In this analysis, all are prisoners of what appears as an iron determination. A few years ago similar views to those cited were very widely expressed by social scientists of a variety of schools. We have already noted, in Chapter 1 (pp10-11), the views of the French Marxist, Louis Althussser,[12] and those of the American economists, Bowles and Gintis.[13] Both allow little or no scope for reciprocal action, through education, on society. A little earlier the well-known reports by both Coleman and Jencks, also from the United States, based on intensive analysis of the existing situation, both concluded that 'schools made no difference' to social structure, or the distribution of life chances.[14] The unfortunate popular conclusion was encapsulated in the phrase 'Education doesn't matter'; education can only reflect and reinforce what actually exists – certainly it cannot and does not motivate social change. To believe otherwise is illusory.

Our focus today is on universities – not on the educational system as a whole. If we take a look at the historical record, I would argue, it is possible to come to quite a different conclusion about the relation between universities and society, requiring at least the adoption of a more flexible view. The role of universities, it may be argued, differs at different periods, and according to different circumstances. There have been times when these institutions – even the most ancient and most sacred – have in fact pioneered (or shall we say, been responsible for) social change; more especially if a university is defined, as it should be, as a community of scholars including students. Can we take an example, first, from a country already referred to; that is, Russia, through now looking back to the nineteenth century?

When the Russian monarchy, early in that century, was concerned to ensure in an economical and tested way the production of administrators and bureaucrats to administer that vast and ramshackle domain, not unreasonably (in the context of the times) they took Prussia as their model, and established in the main cities the equivalent of the German classical gymnasia and, in St Petersburg and Moscow, both universities and higher professional schools (for instance, the famous Medical Academy and others, which, in these cases, reflected the French Grandes Ecoles). The outcome of this policy was, however, hardly that desired. Certainly these institutions did produce the officials and bureaucrats, the doctors, lawyers and military experts that were required. What was clearly not intended was the massive alienation and radicalisation of a large proportion of the students, leading to the great student strikes and related actions of the 1860s.

In *Training the Nihilists*, Daniel Brower analyses this striking social phenomenon, showing clearly that the radicalised students came roughly equally, from all the privileged social classes, including the nobles.[15] In that sense, the Bourdieu thesis still holds – the universities were reproducing existing social relations. But it was the outlook of these students that was transformed through the experience of higher education in the circumstances of the time. Brower describes the social forms and philosophical and social/political outlook of these students, the literature that they used for their own self-education (the French socialists – Saint-Simon, Fourier – the English political economists in particular), and the way this student movement linked with the democratic thinking of the leading group of advanced radicals of the 1860s – Dobrolubov, Belinsky, Chernyshevski and, in exile, of Herzen. Nihilism does not describe the outlook of the students of the 1860s, who were really children of the Enlightenment, deeply concerned with clarifying the nature of moral behaviour, especially as it concerns relations between the sexes, and whose social policies related to such matters as the establishment of small co-operative producer societies, seen as an alternative 'system' in much the same way as the early Owenites established co-operative communities in England some thirty years earlier. All this forms the subject matter of Chernyshevski's *What Is To Be Done?*, a seminal and profoundly influential book which delineated the ideal type – the new man and woman – of the Russian democrats of that time. Later, in an effort to link up with 'the people', these students turned to mass literacy campaigns among workers and peasants (a movement with which Tolstoy was closely connected in his old age). The terrorist policies which followed the failure of these initiatives were policies of despair. But it is worth recalling that Lenin's brother, who participated actively in student affairs in the 1880s, was in fact executed as a result of activities in which he was closely involved shortly after leaving university.

Is there not a direct line of connection between the alienated students of the 1840s, 50s and 60s and the events of October 1917? If the relations between education and society are generally interpreted, by neo-Marxists and others, as ensuring social reproduction, the perpetuation of existing social relations, and therefore stability, does this mean that unintended outcomes no longer occur in this field? That policies of social control always achieve their objectives? What are the lessons, for instance, from the fact that it was sustained and highly organised student initiatives which sparked, and in a sense, led the recent revolutions in both Czechoslovakia and Romania.

But let us now move to a different country, and a different period. Can we cast our minds back to the eighteenth century (that period of stability), and to an ancient and venerated institution – the University of Cambridge. Can we find anything there that may cast light on our thesis?

The answer must be yes; and this in spite of the fact, well-attested by research, that the social composition of the student body was dominated by aristocracy and gentry, by the clergy and other established occupational groupings. Nevertheless, by mid-late century, the culture of Cambridge was dominated by rationalist thinking – Newtonian physics and mathematics (as well as geometry); by John Locke's necessarianism, the philosophic basis of which was laid in his *Essay on Human Understanding* (required reading, by the way, for the so-called 'non-reading man' such as, for instance, William Wordsworth, strange as this may seem); by David Hartley's development of Locke's thinking in his path-breaking *Observations on Man*, published in 1749; by the values of Ciceronian republicanism which formed the staple of classical studies, and by other works of a like character. Clearly Cambridge's official culture (if one may use the term) differed profoundly from that at Oxford. From mid-seventeenth century a conscious modernisation of the curriculum had taken place, the ground base of which lay in the work of Newton and Locke. The nature, ethos and life of the place bears little relation to that of Gibbon's port-swilling Oxonians of the same period (though we should remember that the great historian spent only one year at Oxford when aged fifteen). Nurtured on such literature, and, of course, endless talk and discussion (particularly among students and some younger dons), there arose towards the end of the century a strong dissentient movement at Cambridge aiming at reforms both within the university itself and within society as a whole. The main internal targets were examinations (since these were corruptly determined), and especially the religious tests then demanded whereby, it was held, the university was committed to outmoded and indeed thoroughly disreputable standpoints on religion and philosophy. It was here that the tension was greatest.

Perhaps we can focus on this movement of ideas just for a moment, and on the central issue where conflict was sharpest, having widespread implications. In his fascinating study of this period, entitled *Wordsworth's Cambridge Education*, Ben Ross Schneider argues that the Cambridge dissentients of that period held that 'if reason were to hold sway in men's affairs it must have complete freedom to operate'. Hence their petitions to Parliament in 1771 and again in 1791 against existing religious tests in the country at large, as well as their appeals (Graces, they were called) in the University Senate in 1772 and 1787, against those imposed by the University. Cambridge pursuits, as one of their number pointed out, were especially conducive to free thinking:

Mathematics ... which have long been the prevailing study at Cambridge, are of a bold and searching spirit. Unaccustomed to admit anything in haste, habituated to reason from principles invariably true and universally acknowledged, contemplating the analogies of nature, and proceeding in the way of science, the mathematician embraces no opinions at random, how venerable soever their antiquity, and though sanctioned by the highest authority. He examines coolly, debates with candour, and concludes with caution. Such is the natural process of *Philosophy*; and such has been the effect of the philosophising spirit at Cambridge – and real Religion calls no man, *Master*.[16]

But the mathematical thinkers at Cambridge, 'in search of room for their grand new philosophies, came against a wall of statute'. This was embodied in an Elizabethan edict called 'de Concionibus'.

We do forbid that any person shall, in any sermon, in drawing out any thesis, in public lectures, or in any other public manner, within our university, teach, or treat of, or defend any thing against the religion, or any part of it received and established in our kingdom by public authority ... Whoever shall do the contrary shall, upon the order of the Chancellor with the assent of the major part of the heads of colleges, retract and confess his error and temerity.

Most of the Cambridge dissentients were by this time Unitarians. Under this and other statutes still in force, they could not argue their new theology in any public way, either through lectures or publications. The situation, they felt, was intolerable. The main centres of the reform movements among dons were the great colleges of Trinity and St John's, but included Christ's and (at variance with its more recent character) Peterhouse, joined later, and with special force, by Jesus College. As already mentioned, petitions and Graces against religious tests were consistently presented to the Senate as also to Parliament in the 1770s and later. But the reform movement cast its net a great deal wider. Its adherents approved and encouraged the American revolution and, shortly after, the early stages of the French revolution; they were active in the movement for Parliamentary reform in the early 1780s and, of long-term significance, some of them took a prominent part in forming and continuing the English reform societies – a direct involvement in political activity.

All this led to a movement of some strength within the university – climaxing, perhaps, in the almost farcical trial of William Frend, the Jesus College Unitarian convert, for blasphemy (he was charged under the edict just quoted). This is where Samuel Taylor Coleridge had his blooding as a youthful activist – the sometimes imaginative tactics utilised by Frend's student supporters included emblazoning the slogan 'Liberty and Equality' through the use of gunpowder trials on the sacred lawns of Trinity. Several of those involved linked closely with the nascent and radical working class movement in the Corresponding Societies of the early 1790s – for instance, Horne Tooke of St John's or, in the case of Capel Lofft of Peterhouse, with the Constitutional Information Society's political education campaign. Thomas Fysshe Palmer, of Queens', assisting a society composed of weavers and mechanics, fell foul of the Scottish judges and, at a famous trial at a moment of political crisis was sentenced to seven years transportation as a felon, being shipped in irons to New South Wales, never to see England again. There are very many more who might be mentioned. Schneider, who has the credit of first bringing this whole movement to light, claims that 'the English Popular movement for universal franchise and annual Parliaments that followed the French Revolution was in great measure a Cambridge creation'.[17]

I think he has made his case. As he points out, this movement was for a long period virtually hidden from history, largely because, when the biographies of those involved came to be written during the 19th century, many were 'careful to suppress the youthful errors of their subjects', especially those of 'the unfashionable Jacobinical variety' – only some traces of them 'slipped through the censorship of a discreet century'.[18] More recently, thanks to studies like Schneider's (where he had the help of Godwin's diary only recently made available), that by Nicholas Roe concerning both Coleridge and Wordsworth's youthful radicalism, and especially Richard Holmes' magisterial first volume on Coleridge published recently, a great deal more is known of this movement than in the past.[19]

So, what has been excavated there is the story of a movement of considerable significance, whereby the thinking accruing within a specific culture spread far and wide outside the university, developing an outlook and programmes which, if at that time successfully suppressed, were to emerge later on a national scale with considerable force and which, by this means, played a part in bringing about both social and political change. Although themselves representative of established forces in society, those involved deliberately set out to initiate social, political and indeed cultural transformation. As Schneider puts it, summing up at one point:

> Thus, with Cambridge disinterestedness and in the name of reason, the Cambridge dissentients went to war with the *status quo*.[20]

May we now move roughly a century forward – and fifty miles west – to Oxford (now somewhat reformed since Gibbon's days), to look at what proved to be quite dramatic happenings at Balliol, now undoubtedly the leading college at that university? For it was here that, at this time, a new Weltanschauung was being fostered which, for a time, carried all before it, and certainly closely influenced social and political action. This outlook, in sharp contrast to the Cambridge rationalism of the late eighteenth century, was an Anglicised version of German Philosophic idealism. Its prophet, if that is the right word, was Thomas Henry Green.

This standpoint, as formulated by Green, emerged at a point when what might be called religious (or Christian) fundamentalism was suffering a severe erosion, from two sources in particular: critical historical scholarship on the one hand, and the impact of science and scientific analysis on the other. It is, today, difficult to convey the intensity of the crisis of conscience that overcame intellectuals and others with the decline of religious faith in its traditional forms, coinciding with the emergence of new, sharp social divisions, and specifically the deteriorating and often horrific condition of the urban poor. It was Green's search for a cohesive philosophical system, religious in character, but one that embodied (or rose above) these critiques, and could act as a bedrock (and guide) for human action, that led him to the German Idealists. From his very involved philosophy, which he himself articulated with difficulty, Green fashioned what we would now call an ideology which celebrated 'active citizenship' as 'the highest attainable morality'.

'Between 1880 and 1914', writes Melvin Richter, at the start of his study of this movement, 'few, if any, other philosophers exerted a greater influence upon British thought and public policy than did T.H. Green'. Both James Bryce and Herbert Asquith 'have testified that Green's Liberal version of Idealism superceded Utilitarianism as the most prominent philosophical school in the universities'. Green, he goes on, 'converted Philosophic Idealism, which in Germany had so often served as a rationale for conservatism, into something close to a practical programme for the left wing of the Liberal party'. From aristocratic Oxford 'there came a stream of serious young men dedicated to reform in politics, social work and the civil service'. Many of them 'were to spend their lives in improving the school system, establishing settlement houses, reorganising charity and the Poor Law, and working in adult education. A rich literature of memoir and autobiography attests to the great mark Green left on the minds and lives of his generation. The literary criticism of A.C. Bradley, the economic history of Arnold Toynbee, the view of the history of political thought taken by C.E. Vaughan, Sir Ernest Barker and Lord Lindsay owe as much to Green as did the London Ethical Society, an agnostic organisation outside the Church of England, and the Christian Social Union and *Lux Mundi* movements within it'.[21]

Although in no sense a fluent lecturer, Green's appeal to the students of his day was immense. Alfred Marshall, the economist – hardly given to enthusiasms – described Green's lecture room: 'A hundred men – half of them BA's – ignoring examinations, were wont to hang on the lips of the man who was sincerely anxious to teach them the truth about the universe and human life'.[22] Another recalled that 'for many terms ... I had followed his remarkable lectures with enthusiasm and intense strain ... I can remember that I did not understand a single word as I wrote down the perplexing tangle of sentences furiously and at lightning speed: then in the quiet of my rooms I brooded over them till light seemed to gleam from the written word'. The philosopher, J.H. Muirhead, tells how a passage Green read, later published, had an effect 'nearer to what in the language of the time was called "conversion" than anything else I have ever experienced'.[23] And so one could go on.

Green, and his close colleague Arnold Toynbee, are credited by Richter as putting to rout the Old Liberalism of the Manchester School and replacing, or transforming it into the new Liberalism 'which inspired the social legislation enacted by the Asquith government before war came in 1914' – substituting collectivism for individualism.[24] This claim has been contested, but it remains in essence true. Civic action was, for Green, *the* means of self-realisation – the continuing realisation of the divine in man, as embodied also in human institutions, those of civil society. The rich, or comfortably off (middle) classes could (must) assuage their guilt through positive social action; the aim was 'to moralise the competitive society of capitalism'; this was the basis both of Green's radicalism, and his appeal.

To understand this we need to recall that, in the 1870s and 80s, there took place an important and deep-seated shift in public opinion about the social and economic structure of Britain which was finally embodied in legislation. The origin of this ferment, according to a perceptive observer (Beatrice Webb) 'is to be discovered in a new consciousness of sin ... a collective or class consciousness; a growing uneasiness, amounting to conviction, that the industrial organisation, which had yielded rent, interest and profit on a stupendous scale, had failed to provide a decent livelihood and tolerable conditions for the majority of the inhabitants of Great Britain'.[25]

It was this that provided Green's strategy for reform. The appeal, as Richter puts it, 'was both to the intellect and the emotions ... As a university teacher with a following not confined to Balliol', he writes, 'he first made himself felt in the 1860s. Thereafter no one at Oxford, with the possible exception of Ruskin, rivalled him in his power to stir men from their inherited allegiances and make them aware of how much remained to be done by way of reform'.[26] He himself, very unusually for an Oxford don, was early elected a member of both the

School Board (in 1874) and of the Town Council (a year later) – taking part in and supporting many local associations and activities relating to health, education and (especially) temperance. It is said that he had gone straight from the poll when he had been elected a town councillor to lecture on *The Critique of Pure Reason*. Green had, of course, acted as Assistant Commissioner for the Schools Inquiry Commission in the 1860s, writing many detailed reports on individual schools. He did pioneer work also in adult education. When he died, at the youthful age of forty-six, 2,000 mourners followed his hearse through torrential rain at Oxford.[27] Only after his death did his works appear in published form in large editions, with frequent reprints; his reputation was at its zenith after his death in 1882 up to 1914. Mrs Humphrey Ward's novel, *Robert Elsmere*, was dedicated to Green, who is 'thinly disguised as Professor Grey'. This sold 5,000 copies a fortnight for many months while, she claimed, 'hundreds of thousands have been circulated in sixpenny and sevenpenny editions.' Half a million were sold in the United States within a year of the book's publication. This novel which, as is well known, greatly troubled Mr. Gladstone, popularised Green's teaching and outlook and still brings to life in a dramatic form the social and religious realities of that time.[28]

Green's Idealist philosophy, which carried all before it up to World War One, did not survive the critique levelled first by the Cambridge philosophers Russell and Moore, and later by the analytical school responsible for the 'revolution in philosophy'. Further, by this time, circumstances had radically changed with the emergence of bureaucratised (or state provided) welfare services on a large scale. Though Green certainly supported state intervention in the field of health and education in particular, following World War One there was no longer the same scope or call for *voluntary* action of the kind that drew young graduates to the Settlement movement in East London in the 1880s. So Green faded into obscurity – in several senses now a forgotten man, though Peter Nicholson, in *The Political Philosophy of the British Idealists* (1990), presents a sympathetic analysis of his outlook. In terms of my topic in this essay, Green and the group around him – A.C. Bradley, R.R. Nettleship, Arnold Toynbee and many more have a serious significance. Through them, as through the Cambridge dissentients of the late eighteenth century, the university reached out to a wider world; and with something of a transforming power. In spite of the various (and fairly typical) social origins of their students, they also were at war with the *status quo*.

If we look at the historical record as a whole, we have to accept that universities have tended to be conservative institutions, both in terms of their own inner procedures and of their impact on society as a whole. That today they still have this character is the burden of Charles Carter's indictment in *Higher Education for the Future*, published ten years ago (at a rather crucial moment), though there he sets out a programme for change.[29] I have sought only to show that it can be otherwise – that there have been times when, in spite of their historic connections, initiatives, emanating from universities, have spread far and wide through the body politic – particularly at moments when they, or their representatives, have deliberately sought this wider market. T.H. Green, when an Oxford don and Professor of Moral Philosophy at the university, deliberately sought membership of the local school board and city council, endeavouring to make a practical contribution directly in line with his agonisingly wrought philosophical symbiosis. Thomas Fysshe Palmer suffered deportation in a generous attempt to assist the immediate struggles of artisans and mechanics. Both reached out to a wider world in an attempt to realise what in the end were strictly moral principles hammered out within the college cloisters.

I have presented two forms of analysis in tackling this question, the one sociological, the other historical. It is perhaps not all that surprising that each comes up with a different answer. The sociologist necessarily and rightly focusses on analysis of the existing situation; on the other hand it is specifically the historian's province to analyse and, hopefully, to explicate change. Unless wedded to an iron determinism – and these are few – the historian sees human action as central. Men and women are not the puppets of external forces quite outside human control. However accurate, let's say, Pierre Bourdieu's analysis may be, the situation it reveals is open to change through human action. Indeed it is surely clear that his own research and publications, by laying bare what he sees as the reality beneath the appearance, are intended to provide the weapons for precisely such action.

Perhaps we can return now, if briefly, to the crucial question of access, with which I began – to those 'ripe and hopeful wits' as they were described three hundred years ago, who are 'utterly lost for want of education'. Today, while geographical location still plays an important part, the chief obstacles to their advancement are both class and gender based. Thirty years ago, in 1961, W.D. Furneaux published, in *The Chosen Few*, the results of his study of selection for universities. He specifically drew attention to 'The extraordinary stability in the picture of differentials in social class attainment, not only over the past ten years but over the past fifteen or twenty ... In fact', he added, 'we have a class structure which, as things stand, is virtually self-perpetuating ... Unless we have done something about initiating social change', he concluded, 'then we shall be in the same position in fifty years time as we are now'.[30]

These have proved, at least after thirty years, to be prophetic words. It is well known that the Robbins and post-Robbins expansion has done nothing to alter class differentials as regards access to universities and higher education generally (though gender discrimination has been modified). Sir Claus Moser, among others, has recently dramatically drawn attention to the fact that Britain is today at or near the bottom of the league tables on almost all the crucial indicators measuring the state of education – and very specifically in provision for the key sixteen to nineteen age group which is essential both for a healthy flow of recruits into higher education and as the means by which the present excluded sections of young people may be prepared for it. We are in danger, Moser warned, of becoming 'one of the least adequately educated of all the advanced nations'. 'Major deficiencies' are undermining the country's well-being with 'dire consequences' for the future. Neither the government's education reforms nor the Labour party's proposals, he argued, sought to reverse this malaise. Neither were attempting to make the required 'leap' in priority, quality and vision. That is why he proposed that a Royal Commission be given the task of conducting an all-embracing, visionary yet realistic review of British education.[31]

You may remember that Moser's proposal was rubbished, almost instantaneously, by a member of the government who claimed that what was needed was the imposition of a market solution which would put everything right and ensure that we entered the twenty-first century with confidence.[32] But this is hardly convincing. Present circumstances are not only socially unjust, they perpetuate the wastage of ability the country badly needs, and on a massive scale. To give free scope to market forces is unlikely to rectify a situation which is in danger of becoming a social disaster. The problem of the sixteen to nineteens, and that of radically broadening access to higher education must both be solved – both cry aloud for deliberate, planned action based on acute analysis of our present failings, which is what Claus Moser called for. This will involve, as far as higher education is concerned, an expanded but differentiated, flexible but unified, pattern through which current divisions between institutions can be broken down or at least modified;

one for which, for instance, the Lancaster pattern of relating orbital institutions (as Annan put it) can provide a model – a pattern probably utilising the modular system allowing credits and transfer, and including both full-time and part-time study. Perhaps there is also a central place for the two-year colleges for which Charles Carter argued, based on the American community college pattern.[33] It is in relation to issues of this kind, in the field of higher education anyway, that Moser proposed intensive discussion, analysis, planning and action. Here lies a hope for the future; one by which consciously directed educational change would itself contribute to social change.

Such actions could break down the exclusiveness of existing educational forms – the bane of English education – and so encourage the release of human potential in a quite new way. Through these means the leading institutions could reach out in new ways to society at large, as both the Cambridge dissentients and the Oxford Idealists attempted to do – and in each case with long-term success. Maybe in a similar lecture a century hence, the early development of such a pattern here in the North-West region will be cited as the origin of the new break-out. This, in spite (or perhaps because) of present discontents, is clearly building up a head of steam which contemporary obscurantism and ad hoccery will, in my view, entirely fail to contain. Though the clouds appear to be massing ominously overhead, here, then lies the silver lining that brings hope for the future.

Notes

[1] Joseph Thompson, *The Owens College: Its Foundation and Growth*, (Manchester 1886), pp 512-5.
[2] William Wordsworth, *The Prelude*, Book Fourth, lines 1-16.
[3] Noel Annan, *Our Age* (London 1990), p376.
[4] Hastings Rashdall, *The Universities of Europe in the Middle Ages*, 1895, revised edition by F.M. Powicke and A.B. Emden, Vol 1, *Salerno, Bologna, Paris*. (Oxford 1936), pp195-7.
[5] Brian Simon, 'The student movement in England and Wales during the 1930s', see pp103-124.
[6] Pierre Bourdieu and Jean-Paul Passeron, *Reproduction in Education, Society and Culture*, English edition (London 1977).
[7] N.G. Annan, 'The Intellectual Aristocracy', in J.H. Plumb, ed., *Studies in Social History* (London 1955), pp241-87.
[8] E.G. Sandford, ed., *Memoirs of Archbishop Temple by Seven Friends*, two vols. (London 1906).
[9] F.A. Iremonger, *William Temple Archbishop of Canterbury: His Life and Letters* (Oxford 1948), p38.

[10] Robert Skidelsky, *John Maynard Keynes, Vol 1, Hopes Betrayed, 1883-1920* (London 1983), pp11-12, 21-2, 72-3, 131-2.

[11] Sheila Fitzpatrick, *Education and Social Mobility in the Soviet Union, 1921-1934* (Cambridge 1979).

[12] Louis Althusser, 'Ideology and Ideological State Apparatuses', in *Lenin and Philosophy and other Essays* (London 1971), pp121-73.

[13] S. Bowles and H. Gintis, *Schooling in Capitalist America* (London 1976).

[14] James Coleman *et al, Equality of Educational Opportunity* (Washington 1966); Christopher Jencks *et al, Inequality: A Re-assessment of the Effect of Family and Schooling in America* (London 1972).

[15] Daniel R. Brower, *Training the Nihilists: Education and Radicalism in Tsarist Russia* (Cornell and London), 1975. This, and the preceding paragraph, is taken from my essay, 'Can Education Change Society?' in Brian Simon, *Does Education Matter?* (London, 1985).

[16] Ben Ross Schneider Jr, *Wordsworth's Cambridge Education* (Cambridge 1957). See also John Gascoigne, *Cambridge in the Age of the Enlightenment* (Cambridge 1989), especially Chapter 7, 'The eclipse of Whig Cambridge'; and Frida Knight *University Rebel, the Life of William Frend, 1757-1841* (London 1971).

[17] Schneider, *op.cit.*, p133.

[18] *Ibid.*, p143.

[19] Nichols Roe, *Wordsworth and Coleridge, The Radical Years* (Oxford 1988). Richard Holmes, *Coleridge, Early Visions* (London 1989).

[20] Schneider, *op.cit.*, p114.

[21] Melvin Richter, *The Politics of Conscience: T.H. Green and His Age* (London 1964), p13.

[22] *Ibid.*, p14.

[23] *Ibid.*

[24] *Ibid.*, pp267, 291.

[25] Beatrice Webb, *My Apprenticeship* (London 1926), pp179-80, quoted in Richter, *op.cit.*, p135.

[26] Richter, *op.cit.*, p293.

[27] *Ibid.*, p372.

[28] *Ibid.*, p28; for the Gladstone episode, Mrs. Humphrey Ward, *A Writer's Recollections* (London 1918), pp228ff. Gladstone wrote a 'thunderous 10,000 word denunciation', 'Robert Elsmere and the Battle of Belief'; see John Sutherland, *Mrs Humphrey Ward: Eminent Victorian, Pre-eminent Edwardian* (Oxford 1990).

[29] Charles Carter, *Higher Education for the Future* (Oxford 1980), see especially pp142-5.

[30] W.D. Furneaux, *The Chosen Few: An Examination of Some Aspects of University Selection in Britain* (Oxford 1961).

[31] *Education*, 24 August 1990; *Independent*, 21 August 1990.

[32] What has been lacking from British education, Mr. Fallon (junior Minister) was reported as saying, in *Independent*, 23 August 1990, is 'the discipline of the market-place', 'the power of the customer', and 'the engine of competition'.

[33] Carter, *op.cit.*, pp46-7.

7: The Student Movement in England and Wales During the 1930s*

December, 1986, when this paper was given to the History of Education Society, was an appropriate moment to recall the student movement of the 1930s. Because it was, in fact, almost exactly fifty years earlier, on 28 December 1936, that John Cornford, fighting on the side of the Spanish Republicans, was killed on the Cordova front in Spain – the day after his 21st birthday. John was a brilliant Cambridge student who had just gained a starred first in history, the son of the Professor of Classics at that university and of the poet Frances Cornford, a great grandson of Charles Darwin, and already a political leader who had shown great courage and determination. His death symbolized for many, then and since, the close involvement of students in the ominous and threatening political developments of the late 1930s. It also served as a catalyst. In those circumstances it was increasingly difficult to stand aside.

But, it could be argued, this was just one action by one young man. Was there, in fact, anything that might be called a 'student movement' in those days? And if so, what form did it take? How did it express itself?

In *The Rise of the Student Estate in Britain*, Eric Ashby and Mary Anderson argue that there certainly was such a movement; this is the

* Delivered to the History of Education Society, December 1986. The author was President of the National Union of Students 1939-40.

only historical account I know that traces its evolution through the difficult years of the 1920s and early 1930s to a powerful emergence from the mid-1930s through to the early 1940s – a period which saw, as they describe it, 'a crescendo of useful activity' which finally put 'the student estate' on the map, with radical proposals for university reform and claims for student participation in government outlined in the final document produced by the National Union of Students in 1944.[1] The phenomenon is defined by the authors as that of 'a corporate student conscience' which developed specifically in the late 1930s and found expression, in their account, in and through the activities of the NUS, which formed the focus, at this time, of many of the actions, movements and thinking with which they are concerned. But this, in a sense, may be regarded as a partial view. The student movement of the 1930s was more broadly based than this account would allow. Oxford and Cambridge, for instance, had no all-university Student Representative Councils which could then affiliate to the NUS. Their students could not, therefore, generally participate in the decision-making process within the NUS. Yet it was at *these* universities in England that a 'student movement' was, perhaps, most clearly visible and influential.

The 1930s, however, certainly saw a considerable growth and strengthening of national political student organizations, particularly those of the left, and of various forms of activity at grass roots level, throughout the universities. The transformation of the NUS nationally at this time (due to its elective constitution) was both the result and the reflection of a transformation *within the separate constituent organizations* – the mass of the universities and colleges. The 'corporate student conscience' to which the NUS gave expression, was based on a widespread movement of opinion, and activity, within the Student Unions or Student Representative Councils, where young men and women who increasingly reflected a new radical outlook were now being elected to leading positions.

Ashby, correctly in my view, isolates two prongs in the student movement of those years – or, shall we say, two main areas of specific concern. These were, first, a widespread critique, which developed with extreme rapidity in the years 1937-40, of the nature and purpose of university education – together with the formulation of proposals for change in its content and form, and in terms of its management and control. What kind of people were the universities aiming to turn out? Were they to be broadly educated, autonomous thinkers and actors, prepared and motivated to place their knowledge and skills at the disposal of society? Or were they, to put it in the jargon of the day, to be cabined and controlled – that is, narrowly specialised – to be prepared as fodder for the ruling interests in what was now widely perceived as an increasingly decaying society. Another aspect of this critique of universities was an increasing concern with the very material issues of health, student facilities and scholarships, together with the concept of student rights – the autonomy of student unions, control over finances, freedom for political societies and debate (sometimes banned at that time), and participation in government.

All this formed one prong of the 'movement'. It led to inquiries and reports, carried through and drawn up by student unions, and presented to the authorities of nearly every university and college in the country – including both Oxford and Cambridge.[2] It was this prong that culminated in the reform programme of 1944 referred to earlier. Looking back on it, one can say that it was a constructive involvement by students in the critique of their own education.

The other prong – of at least equal, and probably greater importance – was a growing criticism of society (as Ashby and Anderson put it); an increasingly committed involvement of students in social and political issues – in the field of unemployment, the conditions of youth, health, and education generally, and particularly in the field of the struggle against war, imperialism and fascism. Indeed 1933 is a key date for the understanding of this whole movement, with Hitler's accession to absolute power in Germany, and the consequent increasingly clear threat to science, knowledge and culture, the free interchange of ideas, and the prospect of peaceful international development. Basically, the immediate origins of the student movement of the 1930s can be traced to that year.

1933 happened to be the year that I personally went up to university (Cambridge) – after a year at school in Germany when our headmaster was removed and imprisoned by the Nazis literally one day after they gained full power, in March that year.[3] I was closely involved, through the Cambridge University Education Society, in the investigation into curricula and teaching carried through in 1937. In the succeeding year I moved to the Institute of Education of London University to train for teaching, and through Student Union activities there got involved in the work of the National Union of Students. I was, therefore, inevitably (perhaps) closely involved in different aspects of the student movement through the key years. This may make an objective assessment difficult for me to make. The danger may be of attributing too much significance to these events of long ago. However that may be, I welcomed the challenge to give this paper, and will turn now to discuss the forms the student movement actually took (in my perception) in the mid-late 1930s, assisted, if I may here acknowledge it, by the help of four friends of that period to whom I submitted a draft some months ago.[4] I will then conclude with an attempt at an evaluation. What, if anything did the movement actually achieve? What, historically, was its significance?

I

There is a problem of weaving together what Ashby and Anderson call the two prongs of the student movement – concern with the universities on the one hand, and concern with social and political issues on the other. These two foci did in fact meet, and were given joint expression at the British Student Congress organized by the NUS and held at Leeds, late in March 1940; and since they focused on this, Ashby and Anderson were able to present the two as both sides of the same coin. But the more political decisions at this Congress were unusual, and in fact led to some difficulties. The NUS as such was not an organization that could, at that time, take a directly political stance, except perhaps in a most general way. On the other hand the universities, the conditions of students, and teaching, learning, health and welfare certainly were its business; and it was here, and broadening out from here, that the student movement, insofar as it found expression through the NUS, focused its activity.

Another point is perhaps relevant. The universities where the most radical political developments and actions took place were Cambridge, Oxford and the London School of Economics – perhaps in that order. There was, of course, a good deal of activity at other universities and colleges, but it lacked the consistency with which such activity was marked at these three institutions. At Cambridge, for instance, after a struggle within the left, a single socialist organization was formed – the Cambridge University Socialist Club – which united Labour and Communist students, and of course many others. The membership rose rapidly in the late 1930s to a peak of over 1000, out of a total of about 5000 students in the university as a whole. This was a considerable proportion. Well organized, extremely active culturally, socially and politically, the Socialist Club developed what Gramsci would call hegemonic status in the university. No other organization came near it in size, popular support and efficiency – although several other organizations were formed at that time. At Oxford, the Labour Club, also now a united organization, claimed 730 members in 1937, producing its own journal – *Oxford Forward* – to a high standard. At the LSE it was, recalls a student who went up in 1936, 'a time of intense political activity and of mental stimulation'.[5] Here the Socialist Society's membership rose in 1936 from 150 to 250. Later in London, University College and Bedford College also came to the fore.

Branches of the University Labour Federation were established in all the universities throughout the country, though those at the three institutions already mentioned were the largest. The ULF was affiliated to the Labour Party, though containing socialists of all varieties, including Communists. This was due, apparently, to a special dispensation negotiated originally by Arthur Greenwood (then President) – whose son, Anthony, was active at Oxford – by which the Labour Party turned a blind eye to the way in which Communist Party members and others not otherwise acceptable as Labour Party members, nevertheless became so through ULF affiliation.

The University Labour Federation produced a regular journal (*University Forward*) with articles by John Strachey, Michael Foot, Gordon Walker, Stafford Cripps, R.H. Tawney, Nye Bevan, and many other Labour and left politicians. The organization was certainly a force to be reckoned with. But my point here is that, the LSE apart, its main strength lay at Oxford and Cambridge, and these universities were generally not affiliated nor effectively represented in the NUS. It was at these two universities that the more directly *political* movement among students most strongly expressed itself.

In the late 1930s a growing tendency towards convergence between the two prongs of the movement found expression. At Cambridge, for instance, as already mentioned, an inquiry was set on foot in 1937 into the content and character of university education right across the board. Meetings were called for representatives of all the main faculty societies – in economics, English, history, modern languages, mathematics, science, and so on, and, as a result of inquiries then carried through, reports were published and communicated to the authorities – that is, the Faculty Boards. Similar inquiries were set on foot at Oxford. This concern in fact paralleled a similar movement in the modern universities, including London. At Manchester, Liverpool, Birmingham, Reading and elsewhere, the unions officially launched a series of such studies and reports. So, on the educational issues, students began now to speak with a single voice. Although the lack of a representative union or student organization at Oxford and Cambridge remained an obstacle, this period did see an increasing number of Oxford and Cambridge College Junior Common Rooms, which were representative organizations, affiliating individually to the NUS.

At the same time, in the late 1930s, the NUS itself was becoming increasingly involved in social, and to some extent political, issues – in particular, problems relating to youth in general. This period, we should remember, also saw the development of a youth movement which was itself increasingly concerned with social issues, and was drawing together a very large number of voluntary youth organizations in the country, Christian and other. A number of very effective joint activities with other youth organizations were held at this time, in which the NUS took a full part. Chief among these was the 'Youth Hearing' – an inquiry into the condition of youth generally, in which the NUS officially participated and produced a considerable body of evidence concerning the functioning of the educational system, focusing on the variation in opportunity available to children of different social classes. Another was the 'National Parliament of Youth', which revived an old form in order to debate contemporary social and political issues, and in which the NUS fully participated, drafting an Education Bill containing many proposals for reform in education at every stage, from the nursery school to university. These two events were organized in January and March 1939 respectively.[6]

Another area of joint activity was participation in the work of the British Youth Peace Assembly, formed in September 1935. This was established by a wide range of youth organizations, both religious and political, and involved them in a variety of peace activities. Here the NUS worked with the Young Liberals, the Co-operative Youth, the Labour League of Youth, the Young Communist League and the Young Conservatives, together with the YWCA, the Church of England Youth Committee, the Young Nationalists and the Federation of Zionist Youth. The BYPA in fact, organized the 'Youth Hearing'. Finally, in 1938-9 the NUS officially participated in the work and conferences of the World Student Association, which united student organizations from colonial as well as metropolitan countries – for instance, India, Indonesia, China and elsewhere (countries where the students were often involved in revolutionary activities). The organization was a far cry from the International Confederation of Students (CIE), to which the NUS had been affiliated since its origin. This was confined to student unions from the main European countries and, in the late 1930s, was almost totally inactive for reasons too evident to mention.

So, on the one hand the NUS moved towards an increasingly committed social and political stance; on the other, the more directly political movement among students also moved towards a concern for, and critique of, education and university issues. This is why, speaking of the latter part of the period, I think Ashby is right to talk of a 'corporate student conscience' as the main characteristic of the student movement of the 1930s.

II

I will now attempt a wider, possibly a deeper, assessment. What lay behind this whole movement? Of what developments was it the product? It is very difficult to reconstitute the atmosphere and ethos of the 1930s. And the real issue is to reconstitute these in the perceptions of that specific generation of students – those going up to university in, say 1932 or 1933 to, say, 1938 or 1939. These six or seven years precisely cover the generation of 1930s students – at least in terms of the 'student movement'.

A good deal has been written about the 1930s generally – mostly in terms of denigration. More recently a counter-movement has arisen which is attempting to redress the balance. So the job is not easy. Ashby and Anderson attempt a brief explanation of the growing social and political involvement of students:

> The depression, unemployment, fascism, the Jewish exodus, Stalin's Russia, the Spanish Civil War: these stirred the conscience of the young and compelled the more sensitive among them to make up their minds where they stood. And they were prodded by a new generation of writers who displaced Wells and Shaw and Galsworthy including what A J P Taylor calls 'the creation of a new element in the Labour Party: the left wing intellectual'. Their media were the rows of pink-coloured volumes published by Gollancz for the Left Book Club, and the scarifying articles which appeared week by week in the *New Statesman*. Isherwood, Strachey, Laski, Middleton Murry among propagandists; Auden, Day Lewis and Spender among poets; Bernal and Levy among

scientists, carried a more uncomfortable message than the socialists of the twenties.

It was reasons deriving from these developments, say the authors, together with the turn to concern with university reform, that led to a big increase in the support given to the NUS.[7]

One could quarrel with some of the details of this formulation, but in essence it is correct. There was in those years not only a resurgence and reformulation of political analyses by leading figures such as Laski and Strachey (and, one should add, Palme Dutt), but there were also new directions in the field of culture of which the poets Ashby mentioned, and others, were influential, especially among the young. New prophets were also emerging among the scientists – Haldane, Bernal, Levy, Blackett, and again many more. These were the people who were forming the ideological-cultural ethos of the time; and within this, of course, there was an active and energetic development of Marxist thinking and analyses, and the emergence as a force within the student movement, of an organized Communist Party. This pursued the policy of the Popular Front before and (with great energy) after the Seventh World Congress of the Communist International, held in 1935. The Congress defined the policy of the Popular Front as the necessary answer to fascism (and it was surely no accident that Popular Front governments were in fact elected in both France and Spain in 1936).

In his analysis of this period, James Klugmann, a brilliant Cambridge student who died in 1977, starts by stressing 'that there are in history some periods where things hardly move, which seem like plateaus, where, when you look back, having become older, it's hard to distinguish one moment from another'. And, he goes on, 'there are periods of extreme change and struggle and storm'. The 1930s, he says, 'was definitely just such a stormy period'. He cites the events in sequence: 1929, the Great Slump; 1931, collapse of the Labour Government and election of the National Government; that same year, Japan's invasion of Manchuria; 1933, Hitler's accession to power in Germany, struggles against fascism in France, and the Long March started in China, finally reaching Yenan three years later; 1935, the Italian invasion of Abysinnia; 1936, establishment of Popular Front governments in France and in Spain; 1937, renewed Japanese invasion of northern China; 1936-9, the Spanish Civil War; 1938, the Munich betrayal, the invasion of Austria and Czechoslovakia by Nazi

Germany; 1939, outbreak of World War Two. 'There can rarely have been a period in modern history with so many stormy events in so short a time.'[8]

If we conflate this catalogue of international events with Ashby and Anderson's analysis of contemporary social, political and cultural developments, we are approaching an understanding of the framework within which the student movement grew and developed – in terms of the perceptions of the students of that particular, and very specific, generation. An ominous shadow hung over the entire period – war and fascism. There was, after all, a growing indigenous and very aggressive fascist movement in Britain, with a disturbing degree of support in high places. Mass unemployment, industrial stagnation and the dereliction of whole areas contributed to a growing conviction as to the fallibility of capitalism, as well as to an increasing concern with the many social problems that now insistently surfaced, and could hardly be avoided. In this situation the search was for an alternative – for a solution that would ensure 'peace, freedom and social justice', very much a slogan of the time. 'Scholarships not Battleships' was a slogan of the students as early as 1933.

This is why the Spanish Civil War from 1936 was seen as having such overriding importance. And why Day Lewis, in his poem on those who fought in Spain, ends with the words:

> We came because our open eyes
> Could see no other way

And also why Thomas Mann, who had now made his full transition to democracy, felt that 'If the Spanish Republic wins, it would be an incomparable act of heroism for these times.'[9]

III

As early as 1933 a conscious and deliberate anti-war movement had developed in the universities (and, of course, outside) – at Cambridge and elsewhere exhibitions were organized and related activities undertaken. This movement arose from the strong revulsion against war which developed from reaction to the carnage in France and elsewhere in World War One. At Oxford this was the year of the famous motion at the union which so shocked the Establishment: 'This House refuses to fight for King and Country' – a resolution carried by

275 votes to 153. Later attempts to overturn it, significantly failed. The motion was directed against the false face of chauvinistic patriotism rather than being a pacifist declaration.[10]

In November that year there took place the first of a series of Armistice Day marches; at Cambridge the march was physically attacked by a posse of rightist students as it passed Pembroke and Peterhouse Colleges. So some students now had their first experience of publicly defending their standpoint – the slogan was 'Against War and Imperialism', and, among movements contributing to the students' critique, anti-colonialism was now increasingly evident.

Much emphasis has been put by later writers on the impact of the hunger marchers who came through several university cities, including Manchester, Sheffield, Nottingham, Oxford, Cambridge and, of course, London. The marchers were welcomed and cared for in an organized way by the students – in London late in 1936, 500 students joined the march to Hyde Park, symbolizing their rejection of the approach that characterized the majority of their predecessors who, in 1926, actively took part in strike-breaking activities. Propaganda visits to university cities (including Oxford and Cambridge) by Oswald Mosley were also actively opposed by mass mobilizations of the students. Hence a continuous politicization was the order of the day. As with other sections of the population, the Spanish War of 1936 crystallized attitudes and led to a mass of activity which was extremely broadly based, and which included, for instance, the Federation of University Conservative and Unionist Associations (FUCUA) and the Student Christian Movement (SCM) in activity directed at assisting the Republican government. Participation ranged from membership of the International Brigade to support for medical aid, for refugees, and other activities. Students were mobilized to take part in elections in the mining villages in the Rhondda and elsewhere – a deeply formative experience for many.

Each individual student reacted in his or her own individual way to these events. There were, of course, different levels of commitment – and of organization and activity at different universities.[11] But that there was a general awakening of a political and social consciousness cannot be doubted. It was this that led to a shift of direction, and indeed to the transformation of the NUS as the body representative of students in general.

IV

I want now to attempt a closer analysis of developments within the NUS itself, some of which, of course, have already been referred to. By 1930, after a lively first few years following its foundation in 1922, the NUS had, as Ashby puts it 'lost its appeal'. Individual student unions were strong 'but national cohesion was weak' – the 'corporate social conscience of students had not yet been aroused'. An attempt to develop a policy on universities generally 'foundered on the very apathy which had given rise to the attempt'. By 1931 'the NUS was in a depression of morale'.[12]

The revival can be traced from 1933, but it was not until 1937 that things really began to swing. The NUS had traditionally organized an annual congress – an opportunity to discuss whatever issues were thought sufficiently important, but which were *not* part of the decision-making process of the union which (at that time) was confined to council meetings of union representatives, which took place three times a year.

In 1937 the NUS Congress was, for the first time, organized around a contemporary social problem, and one closely affecting students. The topic was 'graduate employment'. In 1935, out of 7500 students of training colleges and university education departments leaving in July, 1300 had not obtained employment by the following December. In other professions the problem was only slightly less acute. The 1937 Congress, attended by 160 students, was a serious affair preceded by intensive inquiries from student unions at most universities, and addressed by several distinguished speakers – among them Chuter Ede and Hugh Gaitskell.[13]

The fact of graduate unemployment (and mis-employment) naturally led to a questioning of the nature and function of the university, and preliminary – and critical – discussions took place on this issue. An important aspect was the growing involvement of individual student unions in the preparatory work for this Congress.

It was perfectly logical for the NUS to organize, in the following year (1938), a full congress on the topic 'The Challenge to the University' – specifically on 'University Life and Teaching in Relation to the Needs of Modern Society'. But by this time things had moved on. In accordance with the new, more democratic sentiment, the NUS had, in 1937, changed its constitution, which till then had quite deliberately restricted membership only to university and university college unions. A drive was now made to recruit training-college students and to encourage the formation of representative unions within them. An Education Committee was set up to mastermind this work and to draw up proposals for educational change generally, which culminated in the NUS Bill on this issue carried, with modifications, at the 1939 Youth Parliament. A Medical Student Association was also established, uniting the medical schools and working on proposals relating to medical education generally. There was also an Engineering Students Association established at this time. (By July 1938, twelve Oxford College Junior Common Rooms were affiliated to the NUS).

Much valuable work was done on student health, then an important and traditional NUS concern, with the publication of an authoritative survey with proposals for development.[14] International relations were strengthened through the attendance of NUS delegates at the two pre-war World Youth Congresses, the first held at Geneva in September 1936 and the second at Vassar in August 1938, as well as through participation in the work of the International Confederation of Students (CIE), and through the recently formed and more representative World Student Association based at Paris (of which James Klugmann was secretary from 1935 to 1939).

Of great importance at this time was a new determination of separate student societies to work more closely together in planning joint activities. Here the student committee of the British Youth Peace Assembly was important, uniting the NUS with five other major student organizations – The Federation of University Conservative and Unionist Associations, the Union of University Liberal Societies, the University Labour Federation, the British Universities League of Nations Society, and the Student Christian Movement, which, at that time, played an increasingly important role in alerting students to social issues from a specifically religious standpoint.[15] This committee jointly published a lively paper, *Student Forum*. This concerned itself with a wide range of political, social and cultural questions, but particularly with issues arising from the war in Spain. Big collections for Spanish Medical Aid, and for food and other necessities were made at all the universities – in both Oxford and Cambridge over £1000 was collected, and other universities were not far behind.[16] In October 1938 Edward Heath, chairman of the University Conservatives, visited Spain as a member of an all-party student delegation. Heath visited the

Ebro front and the British and American battalions of the International Brigade. Of these he wrote, in *Student Forum*,

> One could not help being impressed by men whose faith in their cause was so strong that they had been through – and are still going through – so much for it. Many of those we saw have since lost their lives. It is sad when so many of them are of a type which – whatever their party – this country needs.[17]

Earlier, in July 1938, another student delegation, including a Vice-President of the NUS, visited Republican Spain. On his return the NUS delegate toured the colleges, telling of his experience and encouraging the collection of food for the Spanish people.[18]

The 1939 Congress, which took further the discussions of the previous two years, was held against a background of heightened activity and a wider representation. Urged on by two (especially) of the four speakers invited – Dr Reinhold Schairer (a pungent and enthusiastic Liberal educationalist who had been closely involved in the democratic opposition to Hitler then at the Institute of Education) and Ramsay Muir (also a Liberal politician, Professor of History, and progenitor of the first representative student union to be organized in England – at Liverpool at the turn of the century), this Congress set out a whole programme of activities which were generally of a democratic and anti-fascist nature.[19] Commissions considered student activities both inside and outside the university, international collaboration, and university conditions.

The latter commission took up President Roosevelt's slogan, which struck a chord to which students responded – the universities should be 'fortresses of democracy'. On this specific issue there is a clear difference with the ideology and outlook of the 1960s student movement, where the students' main target was often the universities themselves, then seen as oppressive and to some extent direct agents of the State. In the 1930s there were many heroic stories (and experiences) of resistance to fascism, and to reaction generally within universities – in particular, perhaps, in the universities set up by the Chinese Fourth Army during the Long March and in the workers' universities established in Barcelona and elsewhere in Republican Spain during the Civil War. On the other hand, universities in Germany had failed to make any effective resistance to the Nazi takeover. Universities, then, should become 'fortresses of democracy' in this sense, and this was the basis for the campaign launched by the NUS, shortly after the outbreak of war, under the slogan 'Defend the Universities'. The intentions and character of the Chamberlain Government were viewed by this time with extreme scepticism by, I would say, the vast majority of students; and this was reflected in the outlook of the NUS. But, at the 1939 Congress, the students present insisted that, if the universities were to play their role effectively in a democratic society 'it was necessary that they themselves should be democratically organized'. This meant that 'the elementary rights of freedom of speech ... (and of) representation on suitable committees ... should be recognized'. Finally this Congress recognized 'that the unions have more and more become the leading organization of students, rather than purely administrative bodies, charged only with day to day functions'.[20] This transformation from within the unions was an essential aspect of the student movement in the 1930s – since it was this that allowed the students of that generation to give expression to, in Ashby's words, a 'corporate student conscience'.

The work of the student movement in the 1930s culminated in the British Student Congress held at Leeds for a full week at the end of March 1940. This was still the period of the so-called phoney war, and although certain London colleges had been evacuated, the impetus of student activities over the last two or three years was, in fact, maintained and developed along the lines already described. But the Leeds Congress was a new venture. Organized by the NUS, but in consultation with the British Universities League of Nations Society, the Internal Student Service (ISS), the Student Christian Movement, and the three political student organizations – the University Labour Federation, the Liberals *and* the Conservatives – it aimed to provide a forum for all, of whatever views, within the student movement. It was, in fact, symptomatic of that period that student Conservatives fully participated in all these activities, including, as we have seen, aid for Spain.

The Congress was prepared by discussions, forums and debates held throughout the universities. At Manchester, for instance, twenty faculty, religious and political societies took part in organized discussions on the Congress issues; at Nottingham a local congress was planned to precede the national Congress – it was even claimed that *all* Nottingham students were drawn into these discussion. At Cambridge also, political and faculty societies held preliminary discussions, the aim being to send a representative group of students to the Congress. Similar developments took place elsewhere. The programme of the Congress was agreed by all the national participating organizations. I remember one such preparatory session held by the ISS, with Sir Walter Moberly (then Chairman of the University Grants Committee and of the ISS) in the chair and the historian, Lewis Namier, present. The latter could scarcely contain himself at the thought that the students were to vote a resolution on India after only one day's discussion; but here Moberly's avuncular support carried the day. When under criticism for this and other matters, incidentally, the NUS received strong, if informal, support from Fred Clarke, then Principal of the London University Institute of Education.

The Congress met under the auspices of a number of patrons – friends of the student movement. These included Ernest Barker, Carr-Saunders (then Director of the London School of Economics), A.D. Lindsay (Master of Balliol College, Oxford), and the Vice-Chancellors of Leeds, Birmingham and Manchester Universities. The main speaker (and the only speaker other than students) was H.G. Wells – his message did not go down well with the assembled students. Over 600 attended – by far the largest ever to attend a NUS Congress up to that date – though those organized later in the war reached well over 1000.

The Congress worked in Commissions. For the first three days it considered international, social and political issues; for the second three days, problems of universities and colleges. It concluded with the adoption of a charter of student rights and responsibilities. In view of the radical nature of the resolutions passed, usually by huge majorities, it is worth repeating the analysis made on the basis of questionnaires filled in by 332 of the 600-odd delegates. Of these, 73% came from 'secondary' (i.e. 'grammar') schools, and 27% came from public schools. Their subjects of study covered all the main fields relatively equally. 40% of them belonged to 'one or other' student society, but 60% belonged to *no* student society. In the words of the report, 'those who came to learn, and they were the majority of the Congress, found their ideas changing and were able to free themselves from their fixed ideas and conceptions'.[21] However that may be, the level of discussion in the various commissions was extraordinarily high, while the degree of unanimity achieved was remarkable.

The Congress passed resolutions demanding not only political but also economic equality (by 378 to 19); condemned the system of private production for profit, and called for a planned economy (by 416 to 9). Equal opportunities in education and 'a total reorganisation of the Board of Education and of the systems of training and remuneration of teachers' were called for by 382 to 12; the Congress also condemned the arrest of 100 student leaders of the All India Student Federation (by 426 to 2), demanded immediate independence for India, and pledged 'full support for their struggle for freedom' (382 to 26); Congress condemned imperialism and the colonial system (in a long resolution), by 362 to 23. There were other resolutions but these give the feel of the sessions.

'The remarkable unanimity of the Congress on these questions', runs the report, 'is a striking indication of the direction in which the thoughts and ideas of young people are turning. These decisions were not snap decisions. They were taken after hearing all points of view, and much information on the subjects under discussion.'[22]

The Congress also passed a resolution, by 281 votes to 150 (with 48 abstentions), stating that the continuance of the war was against the interests of every country and that it was the duty of students in all countries to work to end it.[23] In interpreting this resolution, one must remember two things: first, that this was still the period of the so-called 'phoney war', though near the end of it – British troops had not yet been seriously engaged in any area; and second, that Chamberlain was still the Prime Minister, with Halifax as Foreign Secretary, the government still being composed almost entirely of members of the Conservative Party, which had been the dominant force in government throughout most of the 1930s. The resolution marks, to some extent, the alienation, scepticism and mistrust in student circles as to the motives and intentions of the Chamberlain government. There was still widespread suspicion that they intended, if possible, to switch the war against the Soviet Union.[24]

On the universities, the Congress followed up the work of previous years embodied in earlier congresses, and especially the many reports and critiques published by student unions. It is difficult to get across the general conception briefly, but one quotation, concerning curricula, from the report may help. Here the two extreme concepts – that of a strictly technical education on the one hand, and that which makes a fetish of 'knowledge for its own sake' on the other, were both rejected: 'Between these two extremes the student fails to get any understanding of the world in which he lives or the relation of his studies to the social needs of the time.' This leads to 'the feeling of frustration and aimlessness amongst many students and the degeneration of culture into something pedantic and esoteric. The universities should be centres of a live and growing culture which draws on the experience of the past for the purposes of the present and the future and is at the disposal of the whole people.'[25]

The resolutions covered a wide field. Presaging Robbins, the Congress resolved that university education should be available to all with 'the necessary ability'; that the universities should be democratized by means of student representation on all governing bodies, and through 'proper consultation with the representatives of the students on all matters affecting the students'. Curricula which are 'abstract, divorced from other spheres of human activity and knowledge, and unrelated to social needs' should be changed to curricula 'which relate each particular "subject" to all other spheres of knowledge, which show the development of the "subject" in relation to developing social and intellectual conditions, and which make clear its relevance to the needs of society'. A 'radical change' in methods of teaching was called for 'in order to develop the full capabilities and critical faculties of students' – more seminars and discussion groups, individual tuitions, 'and very much less reliance on lectures'. The examination system also needed changing. A whole programme was also worked out, aimed at bringing the universities much more closely in contact with youth, other sections of society, and the people generally; the composition of universities should correspond more closely to that of society generally; and a far higher proportion of working-class students should be recruited and financed, as well as mature students who had experience of work in industry and the professions.[26]

The Leeds Student Congress was both an end and a beginning. It marked chronologically the end of the 1930s, and therefore the end of the hegemony of the particular generation of students whose perceptions, and experience of the world, were formed under the particular influences I described at the start, and in the course of what James Klugmann described as the 'stormy developments' of those years. But it also marked the arrival on the scene of what Ashby calls the 'student estate'.

In 1941, 1942, and again in 1943, the NUS organized congresses attended by a thousand and more. Training colleges and technical colleges were now admitted into full membership (by 1945 there were sixty-six training colleges and technical colleges in full membership, with another seven in association). Representatives of the NUS now had regular consultation with members of parliament, government departments, the AUT and NUT, and the University Grants Committee.[27] All this had its inception in the late 1930s. In 1944 the NUS published a major report on the reform of higher education. This is described by Ashby as 'the first considered manifesto from the student estate, a corporate statement agreed after drafts had been circulated to all constituent organisations of the NUS'. It is, he says, 'a bland, almost apologetic document, with none of the strident tones of Simon's book, published in the previous year'.[28]

Whether the document was bland and apologetic is hardly for me to say.[29] But in any case after the 1930s a new phase opened, both within the NUS and among students generally. The 1940s and 1950s no doubt deserve consideration on their own. The 1960s saw a new student explosion or revolt, international in scope, using methods, and carried through under an ideology, in some ways similar but in others very different from that of the 1930s. But these students were reacting, of course, to different circumstances. This also is a matter for separate study, as might be the relative student quietism of the late 1970s and 1980s. Each generation of students is formed in different circumstances. Each has to find its own specific solution to the problems, tensions and pressures, as well as the opportunities, that face it.

V

What can be said in summing up? How can one evaluate a movement of this kind? Of course it affected only a small number of people – an elite, although one that (unusually) actively rejected the concept of an elite, and worked energetically to transform the situation that produced it. But nonetheless, a quite important section of society.

There are many attempts at explanation of the electoral landslide of 1945 – but perhaps it is not altogether far-fetched to attribute some of the change of atmosphere, allegiance and direction to the movement of opinion among students and youth generally in the late 1930s – reinforced, probably, by war experiences. Later investigations have shown that over 60 percent of those who voted for the first time in 1945 (comprising one-fifth of the electorate) supported Labour; the preponderance among this age group alone, it has been calculated, would have been nearly enough in itself to account for Labour's margin of victory – nearly two million.[30] Many students of those years were in the armed forces during the war – and would have participated, and had their say, in the Army Bureau of Current Affairs discussions made compulsory after 1942 – so their influence might have spread in this way. But, taking a longer view, those who graduated between, say, 1935 and 1942 (to cover the 1930s period) would have been aged around forty, twenty years later, in 1955 to 1962 – that is, coming up to their prime. How influential were they, and what kind of influence would they have exerted through the 1960s – and later?

Of course, we cannot say; changing circumstances nationally and internationally brought about changes in outlooks and attitude. While some, I believe a great many, were probably permanently influenced by the activities and ideals of the 1930s, others later rejected them. There were, however, many in my generation, to take just one example, who would never set foot in Franco's Spain when he was there – and that probably symbolizes a certain attitude.

And what about all the thought and energy put into university reform? Has there been a transformation of the content of education, in teaching methods, in university government, and in the university's function in the locality and in society generally, along the lines pressed for by those students of long ago? Well of course there has been change – and some new approaches, embodied first at Keele in the late 1940s (the one new university established immediately following World War Two), and in the thinking (and at least the original structure) of the so-called plate-glass universities of the late 1950s and early 1960s. Many of those who took part in student discussions on all this in the late 1930s later became distinguished academics (I remember the two representatives from the History Faculty Society who came to these meetings at my university – both became distinguished professors, one a Vice-Chancellor of one of the ancient universities, the other head of a college at the other). So, perhaps, some of the thinking and experience did penetrate the universities over the years. But, as we all know, universities have tremendous powers of resistance!

But perhaps I could end where I began. John Cornford's death, as I said at the start, symbolized the growing commitment of that generation of students to the struggle for peace, for democracy, and for the conditions in which science, culture and education could flourish in the face of the growing menace of fascism and war. The gradual response and growing awareness of students in those days took the form of a mass student movement, increasingly directed to clearly defined aims. This was the expression of what Ashby defined as 'a corporate student conscience'.

There have been student movements before and, of course, after. Schneider's researches reported in *Wordsworth's Cambridge Education* (1957) exhumed a very broad-based movement at Cambridge in the late 1780s and early 1790s, motivated by the radical liberalism of the English Enlightenment. Many activities were undertaken, including events of a quite dramatic character. But this movement was hidden historically for 150 years, since its major participants made no mention of it, or obscured it, in their own memoirs written forty to fifty years later, when circumstances had changed and when the admission of participation in radical activities in their youth might have damaged their reputations.

I think it is important that the character and nature, the extent and breadth, of the student movement of the 1930s should not suffer a familiar fate. I am, therefore, glad to have been invited to give this paper. I am well aware of its inadequacy. It has focused on some aspects of this movement and not on others. I have no doubt, therefore, that it is a very partial account. But I hope it may, perhaps, motivate others to add their perceptions of the story – before it is too late.

Notes

[1] Eric Ashby and Mary Anderson, *The Rise of the Student Estate in Britain* (London, 1970) devotes a chapter (Chapter 4) to the National Union of Students in the 1920s and 1930s, which the authors see as the background to 'The flowering of the student estate' (Chapter 5) in the period after World War Two.

[2] The inquiries at Oxford and Cambridge were carried through by informal *ad hoc* bodies, not by the Unions, which were debating societies only. At Cambridge, for instance, reports were produced by an Inter-Faculty Coordinating Committee set up by a student controlled body – the Cambridge University Education Society.

[3] This was Kurt Hahn, then head of Schloss Schule Salem, near Lake Constance in Bavaria (Bodensee). Hahn was a close friend and adviser of Brüning, an ex-Chancellor of Germany. He had made his total opposition to the Nazi party very clear during the previous year.

[4] These are George Matthews, President of Reading University Students' Union, 1938-9, Vice-President, NUS, 1939-40, Vice President, University Labour Federation, 1938-9; Margot Kettle, Secretary of the British Universities League of Nations Society, 1939-40, Secretary of the NUS, 1940-44; Christopher Meredith, NUS Secretary, Queen Mary College Students' Union, 1937-8, General Secretary of the University Labour

Federation, 1938-40; Betty Matthews, Editor *Student Forum* and *Student News*, 1938-40 (and at London School of Economics, 1936-9, after taking a degree at Rhodes University, Grahamstown).

5 Betty Matthews, letter to the author, 1986.

6 *Year Book, 1939-1940*, National Union of Students, n.d., [1940], 36.

7 Ashby and Anderson, *op.cit.*, 69-70.

8 James Klugmann, 'The crisis in the thirties: a view from the left', introduction to Jon Clark, Margot Heinemann, David Margolies and Carol Snee (eds.), *Culture and Crisis in Britain in the Thirties* (London, 1979), pp13-14.

9 Quoted in Nigel Hamilton, *The Brothers Mann* (London, 1978), p296; see also 288-9, 300.

10 The Oxford motion was debated at other Student unions – at the London School of Economics it was carried with only 30 dissenting in a house of more than 300. See Peter Stansky and William Abrahams, *Journey to the Frontier* (London, 1966), p209.

11 H.S. Ferns, a Canadian higher degree student at Cambridge in the late 1930s, gives one reaction in his memoirs, *Reading from Left to Right* (Toronto, 1983), p118: 'The politicisation of Cambridge in the 1930s is in fact quite easy to explain. Politics at that time was simply the most thrilling, fascinating, and important of human activities. One had to be stupid and insensitive indeed not to take notice of what was going on in the world and to feel at least some degree of involvement. Those who today claim some kind of wisdom because they stood aside and kept quiet were not always the virtuous ones. Quite otherwise.'

12 Ashby and Anderson, *op.cit.*, pp69-72.

13 *Twenty-one Years of NUS, 1922-1943* (National Union of Students, n.d., [1943]), 6; see also *Graduate Employment*, report of the 1937 NUS Congress (National Union of Students, n.d., [1937]), *passim*.

14 *Student Health* (National Union of Students, December 1937). This was subtitled 'The report of an enquiry into University Health Services by the National Union of Students'. 104 pages in length, this was a very thorough study. A supplement was published in December 1938.

15 *Twenty-one Years*, p9.

16 *Ibid.*, p9.

17 *Student Forum*, 19 October 1938.

18 *Twenty-one Years*, p9.

19 *Report of the Annual Congress, 1939* (National Union of Students, n.d., [1939]), *passim*. The 1938 Congress report was entitled *The Challenge to the University*.

20 *Ibid.*, (1939 Congress report), pp29-30.

21 *Students in Congress, Leeds – 1940* (National Union of Students, n.d., [1940]), pp4-5.

22 *Ibid.*, 7. The following comment by a participant, Oscar Buneman, may be of interest; it appeared in the Student Congress Supplement to the Manchester University Union's *News Bulletin* (vol 8, no 8, 25 April 1940):

Many of us went with the intention of hearing H.G. Wells, of having a good time and of enlarging our social opportunities. We came away with a much deeper impression in our minds; the experience of having lived in what may, without flattery, be termed an enlightened community. We had anticipated the sessions and discussions to be stereotyped repetitions of left-wing phraseology and we had intended to cut them like lectures; instead, they became for us the centre and attraction of the congress (as the congress organisers had meant them). Mr Wells was soon forgotten, and the absence of night life in the city of Leeds was amply compensated for by the absorbing daytime occupation.

But all were struck with the high level of the discussions, with their well-informedness and with the genuine attempts which were made by Red, Blank and Blue to come to terms and work out a minimum programme that could be agreed upon unanimously.

23 *Manchester Guardian*, 1 April 1940; the discussion is reported in *Students in Congress, Leeds – 1940*, 19-20.

24 This is reflected in A.J.P. Taylor's analysis of this period, in *English History, 1914-1945* (Harmondsworth, 1970). Of the Finnish campaign, which he compares to 'Gallipoli again, and worse', Taylor writes: 'The motives for the projected expedition to Finland defy rational analysis. For Great Britain and France to provoke war with Soviet Russia when already at war with Germany seems the product of a madhouse, and it is tempting to suggest a more sinister plan: switching the war on to an anti-Bolshevik course, so that the war against Germany could be forgotten or even ended.' The only charitable conclusion, he suggests, 'is to assume that the British and French governments had taken leave of their senses'. See pp571-2, and especially note 3. The Finnish war took place over the winter months of 1939-40.

25 *Students in Congress, Leeds – 1940*, p23.

26 *Ibid.*, p24ff.

27 Ashby and Anderson, *op.cit.*, p86.

28 *Ibid.*, 86. The NUS report was entitled *The Future of University and Higher Education* (National Union of Students, n.d., [1944]), the book referred to is my *A Student's View of the University* (London, 1943). This originated as an official project sponsored by and on behalf of the NUS. The project was abandoned on the outbreak of war and the book completed as a personal statement, the originally agreed title, 'The Students' View of the University' being altered accordingly (see author's foreword, p6).

29 Perhaps I should make it clear that I, personally, had nothing to do with the 1944 policy statement since, from 1940, I was in the army.

30 Paul Addison, *The Road to 1945* (London, 1975), pp267-8.

Part Three

8: The Study of Education as a University Subject in Britain[1]*

First, it may be worth reflecting briefly on education as a university subject – its evolution and character – as compared with other 'subjects', both 'pure' (history, physics) and 'applied' (engineering, medicine, law).

One thing is clear. Education as a specific focus of study did not enter universities in Britain until comparatively recently. It did so as a result of an external demand on the universities – to participate in the professional training of teachers. It was, therefore, a product of the rise of mass systems of education which were brought into being in most advanced industrialised countries as a result of industrialisation and urbanisation. The first university chairs in Britain, as is well known, were established in 1876 in Scotland, perhaps almost fortuitously;[2] but at that time there was no commonly accepted or organised body of knowledge illuminating the field – nothing, in any case, of a scientific nature. It was Alexander Bain, when Professor of Logic at Aberdeen, who published, in 1879, a seminal book entitled *Education as a Science*; but this could do little more than point the way in which the study of education might develop if such an approach became common. This book was certainly influential, but chiefly in the support it gave, both theoretically and practically, to practising school teachers.

* From *Studies in Higher Education*, Vol 8, No 1, 1983.

The closing years of the nineteenth century saw a tempestuous development of educational institutions of various kinds. By this time elementary education had developed as a system, while secondary schooling was on the verge of a similar move. University involvement in the professional training of teachers began in the 1890s in relation to elementary schools. Only after the 1902 Act did attention begin to focus on teachers required by the new system of secondary schools.

So a specialist staff began to be recruited, responsible for training teachers. New institutions and university departments were brought into being; after a struggle, chairs were established and professors appointed.[3] The 'subject' was now gradually embodied in universities, if in a somewhat peripheral manner. (It is worth noting that the departments were crucial to the emergence and strengthening of the modern universities in the first two decades of the century, since their subsidised students swelled the somewhat exiguous student totals.) With this development university norms began to apply, relating to publication and 'research', and, in this manner, a body of knowledge and norms of procedure began to be created.

Evidently, then, education, as a subject of university study, being a 'practical activity', relates more closely, for instance, to engineering and medicine than to other university subjects. The practice of education, even if defined (as Bain did) to exclude anything other than schooling, involves hundreds of thousands of teachers and millions of students. Evidently the scope and focus of study of this process cannot be easily defined nor rigorously enclosed within strict or distinct limits. On the contrary, knowledge from a variety of disciplines is relevant, and has been seen to be relevant from the start. The study of education requires not only a multi-disciplinary approach, as, for instance, is also the case with subjects like politics and geography; but also poses problems of particular sharpness concerning the relation of theory to practice. What, for instance, are the specific features of a strictly educational theory? And from what disciplines and in what manner can theoretical knowledge be advanced? These are the sorts of questions that are relevant to this issue.

Although the purpose of this article is to focus on the last thirty years, during which a massive expansion of education as a university subject took place, a few words should be said about the early period since this set the pattern for later developments. In a lecture delivered in South Africa in 1918, Fred Clarke, later Director of the London University Institute of Education, and throughout his life a seminal thinker on this topic, bemoaned the fact that those concerned with the study of education at universities had failed to advance the subject as it deserved. The reason for this, he claimed, was that originally their main function was seen as the preparation of elementary school teachers; official regulations (from the State) being designed to prevent the development of any kind of critical awareness on the part of these students. The professor's job at that time was seen as largely administrative. Even when, from the early twentieth century, attention shifted to the preparation of teachers for secondary schools, similar conditions persisted, if not for the same reason. Time spent travelling round the country watching students teach, with the focus on induction specifically into subject teaching, left little time or energy either for serious research, or for study and reading. As a result, to extend Clarke's analysis, the actual conditions in which the bulk of staff of education departments operated functioned to restrict the vision of their members, and did not allow the proper development of educational studies as a university subject. It was, no doubt, partly as a reaction to this situation that some of the new universities founded in the late 1950s and early 1960s deliberately established education departments without this responsibility – an example being the Department of Educational Enquiry at Lancaster.[4]

One important exception to this rule may, however, be noted. In Scotland the training colleges, which play an important role in national consciousness, successfully fought for a monopoly of teacher training so that (with the exception recently of the University of Stirling) all graduates receive their professional training in such colleges. University education departments in Scotland (at Edinburgh, Glasgow, Aberdeen and Dundee) do not themselves undertake the initial training of teachers in the same way as the bulk of their English (and Welsh) counterparts. These have, as a result, tended to remain small (in comparison with English departments) but, since they have concentrated, and still do, on advanced studies (higher degrees and diplomas), these departments enjoy the conditions that Clarke regarded as essential for the advance of educational knowledge.

One further introductory point may be made. The bulk of university study and teaching in England and Wales has (historically) been directed at graduate students undertaking the one year course for what is now known as the postgraduate certificate of education (PGCE). This course functions within severe constraints. Since graduate students have to be inducted into the actual job of teaching (and this involves the equivalent of one full term's teaching practice in the schools), there is time only for an elementary introduction to the study of education; little study of an 'advanced' character has been possible. These conditions operated from the start of university departments in the 1890s until comparatively recently – certainly up to the end of World War Two.

This situation began to change from the 1950s. There were, perhaps, two main reasons for this. One was the expansion of university departments which related closely to the concomitant, and massive, growth of the school system in terms of sheer numbers of pupils and teachers. Another was the establishment, following the McNair Report (1944) of Institutes of Education in all the main universities in England and Wales (except Oxford and Cambridge). These had primarily an in-service function, but also brought the training colleges (as they were then known) into a much closer relation with the universities than had previously been the case – further they were initially directly funded by the Ministry of Education, and had a research function built in. Here then was a new source of staff concerned with the study of education (and free from initial teacher training). Following the Robbins Report (1963), most universities fused their departments and institutes to develop 'Schools of Education'. This allowed an infusion of staff who were not 'method' lecturers (subject specialists), many of whom had been engaged in research, and a new and much greater flexibility in the deployment of staff than had been the case earlier. Concentration on specific sub-specialisms in research and teaching now became possible. Related to this, the new and massive expansion of the teaching profession in the 60s created a sudden demand for College of Education staff who required some form of induction into their new jobs, now being defined anew (see below). This concatenation of circumstances, together with the establishment of many new universities, led to a big increase in the provision of advanced courses by university education departments – both diploma and higher degree.[5] Such courses, covering relevant specialisms, meant that now, for the first time, serious study and teaching on a university level was taking place across the field of education as a whole. The content and character of such teaching will be discussed below. What is worth noting at this stage is the comparative recency of such developments – now, of course, threatened, like other university studies, by the radical measures of the present government.

If, so far, I have focused on background considerations, the way is now clear for a closer look at the content of study and teaching at universities. This can best be refined into four periods; first, the early phase, from the 1890s to 1914 or thereabout, when the prevailing theory can best be defined as an eclectic version of Herbartianism. Second, the inter-war phase, dominated by Percy Nunn with the emphasis on individualism and resort to biological explanations of human development compatible with the rise of psychometry (mental measurement) as a 'science'. This phase projected into the 1950s but was superseded by a sociological tendency manifested in the work of Karl Mannheim and Fred Clarke in particular which may be described as a third phase. Radically new developments took place from the early 1960s with the redefinition of what was involved in educational studies by the 'new' philosophers (those involved in the so-called 'revolution in philosophy' based on linguistic analysis) – a trend to which we shall devote considerable attention. This phase was marked by the partial supersession of what had come to be regarded as traditional studies relating to the psychology and history of education by the new disciplines of philosophy and sociology which, as is well known, recorded a remarkable advance from the early 1960s. It may be that a fifth phase is now apparent, the contemporary concern with classroom studies marking a new interest in what may be called 'pedagogy' – an important aspect of teacher education which seems to have suffered a remarkable neglect historically in Britain.[6]

Before the universities entered the field, publications relating to teacher education (and related studies in training colleges) had tended to focus very specifically on the craft of teaching. The many student manuals produced in the 1880s and 90s, for instance, were concerned with the practical application of a general theory of learning, usually derived from Bain's influential book referred to earlier, and in turn based on Locke's philosophical position and, in particular, its application to education through the elaboration, by David Hartley and others, of associationist psychology. This outlook was generally optimistic – Locke held, it will be remembered, that nine parts in ten of what a man (sic) became was due to his education and upbringing. There is no space here to discuss this interesting phase further, except to note that, since this time, what may be called strictly 'pedagogical' studies have not flourished. It was at this time that the universities entered the field, and a broader and perhaps more 'scholarly' perception of what was involved in the study of education gradually made headway. The concern with theory, however, which this perception involved, carried

131

with it the danger of losing touch with practice.

However, it was with the now rapidly developing system of secondary education that the universities were mostly concerned. These new schools required a theoretical underpinning for the teaching process. The main source for this theory was found in the teachings of the German philosopher-educationist Johann Friedrich Herbart, whose main works had been published early in the nineteenth century, but whose ideas had been taken up and adapted to the problems of mass schooling in Prussia by a series of distinguished university educationists of whom Rein of Jena, was the latest and perhaps the best known. The Herbartian system, as developed by his followers, was highly systematic in terms of teaching (with its five 'steps' for each lesson), was based on a modified theory of associationism, and was, therefore, basically optimistic in terms of its assessment of the power of education to influence not only intellectual development but also character and moral outlook. Many of the leading early professors of education in Britain declared themselves to be Herbartians, wrote books popularising Herbart's outlook, and applied his ideas to the practice of teaching individual subjects.[7] It can hardly be claimed, however, that Herbart's English proponents developed his ideas in any significant way, as perhaps John Dewey may be said to have done in the United States.

Although Herbartianism provided the overall thrust of this early development, other tendencies were also apparent. First, among the early professoriat was a number of distinguished historians of education who made a substantial contribution to knowledge. Among these were such men as Foster Watson, at Aberystwyth, who had studied history under A.W. Ward at Manchester, and whose contribution to the scholarly study of educational history was strikingly original and broad in its scope. Others were J.W. Adamson, of King's College, London, where the Chair of Education was later designated specifically for history; and W.H. Woodward of Liverpool who masterminded the first systematic series of studies on this topic published by the Cambridge University Press. Indeed studies in the history of education, if in the sense largely of the history of ideas, characterised the approach of the Scottish universities, S.S. Laurie, the first holder of the chair at Edinburgh being one of the pioneers. Laurie held the view that 'the study of the history of education in the writings of the most distinguished representatives of various schools of thought is an important part of the general preparation of those who adopt the profession of schoolmaster'. This view of the role of history had already been adumbrated by R.H. Quick in *Essays on Educational Reformers* (1868), and was to remain a main ingredient of education courses up to the 1950s and 60s, when a new wave of historians tended to reject this approach, their main thrust then being to interpret changes in educational ideas and practice in terms of changes in economic and social conditions. By that time the 'great educators' approach had been relegated to the past.

Together with history, psychology came into prominence in teacher education courses from the later 1890s – primarily at first (and for a long time after) in the form of 'child study', an adaptation of the developmental approach stemming from the widespread child study movement in the United States. The leading figure here was James Sully, whose *Teachers' Handbook of Psychology* had been published in 1886. It was Sully who, according to Burt, was 'the first to introduce systematic instruction on child psychology into courses for teachers and students preparing to enter the teaching profession'. If, in his first edition, Sully dealt with mental development mainly in terms of growth of the faculties of the mind, later editions (the fifth was published in 1909) stressed the role of the child's activity in self-development, so linking more closely with the ideology of the 'new education' which now began to make its mark.

This first phase, then, which saw the inception of university studies in education, sees the emergence of psychology and history as the main underlying 'disciplines' applying to education. As regards study of the process of education, the dominant ideology (Herbartianism) was still associationist and so positive (or optimistic) in its outlook. However, this dominance was soon to be challenged by the proponents of the new so-called 'Experimental Pedagogy' – an odd expression relating largely to the growth of mental testing, of related statistical procedures, and their application to education.[8]

The second phase covers the inter-war years which were, in many respects, a period of stagnation (as in the case of the economy as a whole). Nevertheless it can also be seen as one of consolidation in that now university education departments came to a certain maturity after their initial establishment earlier. By then most universities in Britain had such departments, while the London Day Training College, as it used to be known, was transformed in 1932 into the premier university centre in the country in terms of size, quality of staff and professoriat and prestige; it was now a full school of the University known as the Institute of Education. There were at this period some 700 students annually studying for the postgraduate certificate (or diploma, as it used to be called), while advanced courses at London and elsewhere (particularly Leeds, Manchester, Birmingham and Liverpool) were being mounted in specialist areas.[9] In Scotland, also, this was a period of development particularly at Edinburgh and Glasgow, where the B.Ed. (a specialist degree for practising teachers, usually studied part-time) had a continuous supply of students, a high proportion of whom later went on to administrative or teaching posts in higher education. Both departments became known for the rigorous study of education, if in particular of psychometric techniques.[10] It is worth noting in addition that the Scottish Council for Research in Education was founded in 1927, some twenty years earlier than the National Foundation for Education Research was established in England.

In terms of the content of studies (or student programmes), however, this period saw little change. The overall transition to the philosophic idealist, biologically orientated, individualist approach has already been referred to. Percy Nunn's *Education: its data and first principles*, first published in 1920, set the tone. This textbook, which ran through some 20 reprintings and two new editions by 1945, was the bible on which the inter-war generation of students was nurtured; though this is perhaps hardly the appropriate word, since Nunn put the major emphasis on nature, being himself a strong proponent of intelligence testing and its application to education.[11] Indeed if any specific ideology or thrust characterised the inter-war period, it is the growing emphasis on precise measurement, together with a strong belief (or better, faith) in the primacy of inborn mental powers. This theoretical emphasis paralleled developments in the schools, where a rationalisation process involving concentration and classification of children was under way. It was this approach which, under Godfrey Thomson and others, dominated the Scottish universities; and which now came to establish its hegemony in psychological and educational studies generally – at the London Institute, for instance, where Nunn was seconded in this field by Burt and later Hamley, at Manchester under Oliver and elsewhere. At the same time one may note the fact that the inter-war period also saw the triumph of the ideology of 'progressivism', at least so far as the primary schools were concerned.

The three main Hadow reports of the period, *The Education of the Adolescent* (1926), *Infant and Nursery Schools* (1931) and *The Primary School* (1933), produced by the Consultative Committee to the Board of Education, which were required reading for many students, all reflected the prevailing 'child-centered' ideology which received support from Nunn's biologically based theories as well as from psychometry which was based on similar assumptions concerning the determining power of innate characteristics.[12]

If, then, there were certain definite and specific developments in psychology (and the emergence of 'educational psychology' as an accepted sub-discipline), so far as teacher education as a whole was concerned, few other developments took place. Although Adamson published his major historical work in 1930 (*English Education 1789-1902*), little was done in this field to build on the work of the pioneers referred to earlier. History of education, however, continued as a main staple of lecture courses for intending teachers (at the London Institute and King's College, by A.C.F. Beales, for instance). Susan Isaacs, on her advanced diploma course again at the London Institute introduced Freudian theories and this initiative was reflected in other departments. Basically the one year course remained an amalgam of lectures on the 'Principles of Education', normally given by the holder of the chair and very much subject to his or her personal predilictions, usually some history (though often still largely of the 'great man' variety), some psychology, now beginning to include an introduction to mental measurement, together with 'method' courses – that is, courses for graduates in specialist subjects on how to teach those subjects. Indeed, as indicated earlier, it was this activity that involved the great majority of staff of university departments, such lecturers normally being appointed after success as a school teacher. The base for serious study of education was, therefore, still attenuated. Indeed failure to come to terms with and engage on such study on the scale insistently required by social developments was the core of Fred Clarke's charge, and challenge, in his short but pungent *The Study of Education in England*, published in 1943 when he was still Director of the London Institute of Education.

Following World War Two, when popular concern for educational advance was enshrined in the Education Act of 1944, we reach the first post-war period of development marked by increasing numbers of students (and therefore staff), and the establishment of Institutes of Education already referred to. Nevertheless, for some time, the scope of studies remained much as it had been in the inter-war years. In the school system, psychometry, now widely regarded as strictly scientific in its methods and procedures, and closely embodied in the system through its use for selection both within and between schools, now gained a dominant position, one reflected in educational studies in the great predominance of psychological studies for higher degrees, a high proportion of which were psychometric in character. The English university centre of this movement (outside London) was Manchester whose higher degree courses were dominated by the study of the theory and practice of mental testing with much attention given to related statistical procedures. Indeed Wiseman argued that, given the predominance of psychological studies, now was the time for a large increase in appointment to professorships of psychologically, and particularly psychometrically qualified personnel.

The main change of emphasis in the late 1940s and 50 has already been mentioned. It was symbolised in the succession of Fred Clarke to Percy Nunn's Directorship of the Institute of Education (London University), though this had taken place some years earlier (in 1936). This marked the beginning of a transition to concern with the social function, or, better perhaps, the sociological role of education. In a seminal book, *Education and Social Change*, published in 1940, Clarke had achieved the first serious socio-historical analysis of the topic in his title. Although in a sense only a sketch, Clarke's insights, and his proposals for future studies, foreshadowed many of the developments in the sociology and history of education that in fact took place from the 1960s on. Noting that writers on education 'show little explicit awareness of the social presuppositions of their thought', and criticising the 'highly generalised principles' of education that figured largely in textbooks as the supposed *determinants* of educational practice, he insisted that thought and practice 'are much more closely conditioned by social realities which are themselves the result of social and economic forces'. Clarke mounted a sustained attack on the way English educationists 'take for granted' traditional structures and procedures. This led him not only to point the need for a new function for educational historians, but also the way to a new approach to the sociology of education which, at this time, was in its infancy. Both had the function of unravelling the real relations, and conflicts of interest, underlying the rhetoric of contemporary discourse. Further, with Clarke's work, inspired partly by Karl Mannheim (whom Clarke involved in educational studies at the Institute during the war), emerged the first clear articulation of the social engineering function of education – an aspect that was to be energetically pursued in the 60s by a Labour Government with the assistance of a new breed of sociologists some of whom (e.g. Jean Floud) had studied under Mannheim at the London School of Economics, and who began to publish their early works in the mid-1950s.[13]

The period of decisive change, however, is that which followed in the early-mid-1960s – the fourth phase of my earlier schema. Some reference to the changed context may be desirable. In sharp contrast to present concerns, this was a period when education was beginning to be seen as central to economic advance (with wide acceptance, by policy makers, of the new, US based, human capital theory). At the same time the move to comprehensive secondary education was getting under way. The fatalistic theories of psychometry were now under sharp and increasing criticism, and were themselves often radically modified by psychologists themselves; in place of these there was now a national concern with the so-called 'wastage' of human abilities. In 1963 the Robbins Committee reported, proposing a massive increase in higher education with a twenty-year plan of advance – a report immediately accepted by the Conservative Government of the day. One year later Labour won the election for the first time for thirteen years – pledged to carry through the white hot technological revolution.

The Robbins Committee proposed advance towards a graduate teaching profession recommending the establishment of the B.Ed. as a means by which college of education students might graduate through a four-year course of study of which education was to be a major component. This implied a much closer university involvement with studies in the colleges than had been the case before, specifically since the degree was to be awarded by the validating universities themselves. In this situation, educational studies, not yet underpinned by any generally accepted theoretical position, required some form of legitimisation (as the sociologists put it). Indeed, generally speaking, the nature and scope for educational studies needed clarification.

The main thrust for this re-thinking came, interestingly enough, from the field of philosophy of education, which had first acquired a named chair – at the London Institute – in 1947. Richard Peters, who had taught philosophy at Birkbeck College, and who succeeded Louis Arnaud Reid in 1962, launched the main attack. Educational studies, he argued, in particular the main general courses offered both at universities and colleges under the heading 'principles of education', were an 'undifferentiated mush'. It was necessary to define as precisely as possible the nature of education as a process, to sort out and re-define the contribution of philosophers to its study, and to clarify the main disciplines on which the study of education was based. 'Such conceptual clarification,' said Peters, 'is pre-eminently the task of the philosopher of education.' Further, it was argued, education was not itself a 'subject' with its own language, forms of thought and concepts. It was best seen as an area of practical activity, one to which various disciplines contributed in the formulation of general principles of action. At a seminal conference at Hull early in 1964, organised jointly by the predecessors of the Universities Council for the Education of Teachers (that is, professors of education) and the Department of Education and Science (for which the initiative came, interestingly enough, from the Department), RS Peters took the offensive, supported by Wiseman (psychology), Bernstein (sociology) and others – the keynote lecture being delivered by the Chief Inspector responsible for teacher training (Gill). What was necessary was the rigorous study of those disciplines which underlay, or contributed to, educational knowledge. Those studying education, particularly at advanced level (and such courses were now proliferating) needed to be inducted into the thinking relevant to the philosophy of education (which should concern itself primarily with conceptual clarification), the sociology of education, now rapidly developing in its own right, the psychology and history of education (though history was the only one of these disciplines unrepresented among the Hull conference lecturers). Thus the model known to educationists as 'the four disciplines' was born.

This model quickly became institutionalised – in a sense it simply crystallised contemporary developments in the field. It was acceptable to universities since, to put it no higher, it seemed to lend academic respectability to the study of education. M.A. courses in the philosophy, psychology, sociology and history of education now mounted at several universities quite rapidly produced a new brand of college lecturers who, having teaching experience, were seconded to universities for advanced study. In the massively expansionist character of the 1960s, when colleges of education expanded three-fold in ten years, these often found employment at Colleges teaching one or other of these specialist sub-subjects now embodied in B.Ed. syllabuses and examinations.[14] At the same time university departments, with their enlarged staff, several of whom were now (with the fusion with institutes of education) freed from 'method' work, also reflected this new conceptual model in their organisation – these specialist lecturers having the dual function of teaching their subject to postgraduates, higher degree and diploma students, and of monitoring the teaching of these new academic disciplines in the colleges.

This period, from the mid-1960s, now saw a proliferation of educational theory – and of educational studies. This is surely partly attributable to the great increase in the number of those professionally involved, at the training level in colleges and universities, in the study and teaching of education. One enterprising publisher, Routledge & Kegan Paul, now started a 'Students Library of Education' which again reflected the philosophers' model. The Editorial Board originally comprised a philosopher of education (Peters), a sociologist (Taylor), a psychologist (Morris) and an historian (Simon), the Board being chaired by Tibble whose interests were catholic; it was later joined by Paul Hirst, a philosopher of education and a leading theoretician of the new model. It may be worth noting that there was no clear place in the original schema for books on the actual practice of teaching (or 'pedagogy') which eighty or more years ago had formed the main staple of publications for students in education. In the outcome an extra section was added, but it was difficult to determine who should be responsible. This is, perhaps, symptomatic of this whole tendency; its implications will be discussed briefly later.

The new conceptual model, as already indicated, called for special attention, in advanced studies in particular, to the four 'basic disciplines' held to underlie or contribute to the study of education. Two of these, psychology and history, had from the 1890s featured centrally in educational studies, even if their content had changed. By the mid-1960s, for instance, psychological studies no longer paid the same attention to psychometry as in the past; indeed this sub-discipline was already coming under severe criticism, while the decline of the actual practice of selection and streaming in the school system meant that it no longer played the dominant role it had earlier. Instead interest now shifted to studies of child development (which had featured earlier) while a new concern with cognitive development focused attention on the work of the Swiss researcher, Jean Piaget, and, if perhaps to a lesser extent, on the Soviet psychologist, Lev Vigotski, whose seminal book *Thought and Language* was translated in the early

1960s. For psychological underpinning in the field of curriculum development, interest turned specifically to the work of Jerome Bruner in the United States, whose studies and research tied in with the curriculum reform movement which took off with considerable force in the early 1960s. Indeed, freed from the straitjacket of mental testing, psychological courses now related more closely to actual developments on the ground in what was essentially an expansionist era. At the same time this period saw a renewal and strengthening of historical studies, the new wave of historians taking to heart Fred Clarke's precepts, in line with the trend in historical scholarship generally towards a new emphasis on social history and sociological determinants. A History of Education Society, reflecting this vigorous development, was established in 1967.

It was the two relatively new disciplines, however, which made the greatest impact: philosophy and sociology. It was not only that the philosophers, for instance, displayed considerable energy, with an impressive output of books and textbooks for students; it was also the case that the definition of the philosopher's role, while restricting this largely to the task of clarification of concepts relevant to educational discourse and action, also outlined a precise but limited field which bore directly on important issues facing teachers and educators generally. The importation of this form of critical analysis, while sometimes appearing somewhat arid and 'academic', nevertheless certainly provided a stimulating addition to courses of educational study. Dearden charts this initial impact, referring to the 'burst of activity' in the 1960s, the 'publications explosion' of that period, and the formation of the Philosophy of Education Society in 1966. However, the main impact on educational studies of the 1960s was probably that made by sociology.

The sudden emergence of sociology as a legitimate field of university study which took place with astonishing rapidity in the early 1960s (in 1963 there were only two chairs in sociology in the country; two years later there were 23) presaged the emergence of the sociology of education as a very important sub-discipline; one which rapidly became established in university education departments through the mid-late-1960s and later (the Open University, in particular, developed as a centre of such study). Since the work of several leading sociologists lay specifically in the field of education (for instance, Jean Floud and A.H. Halsey), and since, in the social democratic consensus of those years there developed a close link between sociology and policy-making at government level, sociology very quickly achieved an important, if not dominating, position in educational studies generally – while empirical (and official government) studies of the late 1950s and 60s provided a mass of data particularly on the relations between social class and educational opportunity which became an important issue at this time. The 1960s also saw widespread interest in the application to education of socio-linguistic studies carried through, in particular, by Basil Bernstein. If the latest review of sociological studies in education reports a certain disarray over the last decade, internal conflicts within the field, as now apparent, have not detracted from the stimulation that studies in this area have provided for educationists generally.[15]

Within this brief review, mention should certainly be made of two further areas of study that have developed over the last two decades, both reaching a certain maturity. Interest in, and study of, the economics of education grew with extreme rapidity in the 1960s closely related (as mentioned earlier) to governmental concern with the implications of human capital theory, and involving contributions by many distinguished economists. This study is now institutionalised at certain universities, as is also the study of administration, proposed long ago by Fred Clarke as an area needing development.[16] At the London Institute there are chairs in both these specialisms, as there are also in two other fields, each involving inter-disciplinary study – comparative education and curriculum studies.

Enough has been said to indicate that the concept of educational studies both broadened and deepened very considerably in the 1960s and early 70s. There was now a closer relation with what might be called 'main-line' studies in universities as a whole. Further these studies were now a great deal more penetrating than in the past – particularly advanced studies of various kinds, which expanded throughout this period. Another stimulating factor was the formation of the Educational Research Board of the Social Science Research Council (1965) prepared to fund fundamental research into education in a consistent way for the first time. Education departments were now becoming more closely linked with systematic research activities – another aspect of university studies which had only marginally been provided for in earlier dispensations. The consequent expansion of qualified research personnel was reflected in the foundation of the British Education Research Association in 1973. In general, then, it can be said that, in the 1960s, university studies in education came of age.

All this was not achieved, however, without some loss. As educational studies became more rigorous and inevitably academic, the historic neglect of pedagogy was accentuated. By 'pedagogy' is meant the theory and practice of teaching. As we saw earlier, in the old School Board days of the 1880s and 90s, strictly pedagogical study formed the central focus of teacher training programmes, taught, in most cases, by the 'Master of Method'. Later this function was relegated, in universities, to the so-called 'method' tutors, who concentrated on this alone. In the new dispensation, method tutors continued this function, but, apart from occasional involvement in curriculum reform issues in their subjects, played no part, generally speaking, in the reconstructed courses in the basic disciplines. The result was a certain separation between theory and practice on PGCE courses at least, in that, with the possible exception of psychology, none of these disciplines was seen to have a direct effect on the practice of teaching. (The counter-argument was strongly put, however, that they had an important *indirect* effect.)

Dissatisfaction arising from this source eventually spurred the Universities Council for the Education of Teachers to mount a thorough enquiry into the PGCE year (in 1974). The outcome, briefly, was that the course for students preparing for secondary teaching should focus very specifically on the skills and abilities intending teachers require for effective teaching in their first job.[17] This marked an important move away from concentration on the 'basic disciplines' as a main focus for this particular course. At the same time the new interest in classroom observational studies, whether those using anthropological techniques or systematic observation using pre-coded schedules, fuelled this movement.[18] The result has been that, over the last four or five years, PGCE courses have tended to shift towards a strictly professional training – a focus on pedagogical issues previously neglected. This trend has also had its effect on advanced studies, with a move towards school based courses in which students are encouraged to investigate and evaluate inner school problems of various kinds – a tendency institutionalised in particular at the Centre for Applied Research in Education at the University of East Anglia and to some extent at the Cambridge Institute of Education.

If the 1960s (and early 70s) can be regarded as a success story, so far as educational studies are concerned, these developments may be put at risk through the reduction of staff in universities and within education departments resulting from present government policy. The health of these departments has depended, to a large extent, on recruiting a wide range of members with a variety of expertise appropriate to an interdisciplinary field like education. Philosophers, sociologists, psychologists, historians, anthropologists, economists, as well as specialists in pedagogy are required to carry through the many responsibilities that have now accrued historically. These range from undergraduate teaching in some universities, the post-graduate education course which provides the bulk of the students, involvement in publicly funded research projects, in-service courses for practising teachers in the vicinity, as well as diploma and higher degree courses (both part and full time) with some doctoral students. Outside the London Institute of Education, with its staff of over two hundred (one hundred and sixty academic, fifty research), most of the modern universities in England (e.g. Leeds, Manchester, Birmingham) maintain relatively large departments to carry out these functions. The Bristol department, one of the most prestigious in historical terms, was first threatened with total closure, then by reduction by half, but seems now to have emerged relatively unscathed. Other departments, while not yet so sharply threatened, are having to shed staff. Though quality, of course, cannot be equated with quantity, such measures inevitably imply a contraction in the scope of studies outlined in this article. Exactly how this will affect developments and in particular the paradigm outlined above, only the future will show.

Postscript (1993)

This paper was published ten years ago, in 1983. Defining the 1960s (and early 1970s) as 'a success story' so far as educational studies are concerned, it warns that the positive achievements of these years may be at risk through the reduction of staff in university education departments as a result of 'present government policy'. Attention was drawn also to the historical neglect of pedagogy which marked these years and the new tendency to move away from the 'basic disciplines' approach towards a focus on a strictly professional training in PGCE courses. This remained a central focus of activity within most university Schools of Education, although a continued growth in in-service, higher degree and research activities was generally maintained over the last decade. This shift of emphasis towards 'practicist' concerns naturally affected the nature of the study of education in this period.

Quite striking changes in the focus of such studies were effected during the 1980s and early 90s. The hegemony of the so-called 'basic disciplines' was certainly broken in the fields of teaching, research and published scholarly studies. The two disciplines which had made a dramatic impact in the 1960s and 1970s, philosophy and sociology of education, both, to all intents and purposes, evacuated the field in the 1980s and early 1990s. An acute analysis of this phenomenon would be desirable but this is not the place. History and psychology (the two original 'disciplines') survived more effectively, at least as areas of study, but certainly neither achieved the primacy they held in the past. On the whole the shift of interest, and emphasis, has been towards the now crucial issues related to school effectiveness, and perhaps especially towards management issues from the individual classroom through the department and school to whole 'systems'. After the passage of the 1988 Education Act there was a strong move towards curriculum studies (but normally subject centred) and assessment and its modes. A tendency to focus on micro, rather than macro issues has also been apparent while problems of gender and race have also been a focus of attention. Oddly, studies in the economics of education have suffered over the last decade, noone assuming the mantle of, for instance, John Vaizey of the 1960s. No very precise direction has emerged in the field of research, but attention should, perhaps, be drawn to a number of critical (but objective) studies of specific government initiatives (eg grant maintained schools, city technology colleges) based on universities.

Late in 1993 new initiatives relating to the education and training of teachers seemed to threaten the now historic involvement of universities with teacher education. It has been this which lay behind the entire development of university studies in education over almost precisely the last 100 years. This move, encapsulated in the November 1993 Education Bill, was strongly resisted by universities as a whole, teachers', parents' and many other organisations and associations. It is too early yet to comment on outcomes.

Notes

[1] An earlier essay on this topic is 'The Development of the Study of Education' by J.W. Tibble in *The Study of Education*, Routledge, London, 1966. A survey of recent developments across the whole field is provided in the thirtieth anniversary issue of the *British Journal of Educational Studies*, Volume XXX, Number 1. This contains articles covering developments in the period 1952–1982 in the sociology, philosophy, psychology and history of education,

as well as in educational administration and the economics of education.

[2] The finance derived from Dr. Andrew Bell's will from moneys left for elementary schools. Following the 1872 (Scotland) Act, the trustees granted sufficient sums from this endowment to create chairs at Edinburgh and St Andrews. See Peter Gordon (editor) *The Study of Education, Volume I, Early and Modern: Volume II, The Last Decade*, Woburn Press, London.

[3] For an example of opposition to this, see 'A Proposed Chair of Education in Mason College, Birmingham' in F. Storr (editor), *Life and Remains of the Rev. R.H. Quick*, Cambridge University Press, Cambridge, 1899, pp373ff. In this case the opposition came from secondary schoolmasters in Birmingham.

[4] Clarke, Fred, *Essays in the Politics of Education*, Oxford University Press, 1923. As many as thirteen of the new universities established from the late 1950s offer education as an undergraduate study, usually in combination with other subjects. Very few of the 'modern' universities do, though the University of Wales is an exception.

[5] In 1981, a total 7188 part- and full-time students were studying for higher degrees in England and Wales, *DES Annual Report 1981*.

[6] The argument in my essay, 'Why no Pedagogy in England?' is relevant to this discussion but will not be repeated here. See Brian Simon and William Taylor (editors), *Education in the Eighties*, Batsford, London, 1981.

[7] For instance, John Adams (later Sir John and first Director of the London Day Training College) whose book, *The Herbartian Psychology Applied to Education*, was published in 1897, see Robert R. Rusk, 'Sir John Adams: 1857-1934' in *British Journal of Educational Studies*, Volume X, Number 1. Other leading Herbartians included J.J. Findlay and J.W. Adamson.

[8] *The Journal of Experimental Pedagogy* was established in 1909 as the organ as this movement. For a contemporary assessment, see J.W. Adamson, The *Practice of Instruction*, 2nd edition, National Society Depository, London, 1912, pp106-129. Early numbers included articles by Cyril Burt and other proponents of mental testing.

[9] In 1937-38 there were a total of 52 full-time and 191 part-time 'advanced' students studying for higher degrees, diplomas, or undertaking research, University Grants Committee, 1937-38.

[10] A fascinating account and interpretation of this development in Edinburgh is to be found in H.M. Paterson's 'Godfrey Thomson and the development of psychometrics in Scotland, 1925-1950', 1975, available in mimeograph; for summary, *Research Intelligence*, BERA Bulletin, Number 2, 1978.

[11] For Nunn, see J.W. Tibble, 'Sir Percy Nunn: 1870-1944', *British Journal of Educational Studies*, Volume X, Number 1. For an acute analysis of Nunn's biologism, see Peter Gordon and John White, *Philosophers as Educational Reformers*, Routledge, London, 1979, pp207-213.

[12] The best studies are both by R.J.W. Selleck: *The New Education, the English Background, 1870-1914*, Pitman, London, 1968 and *English Primary Education and the Progressives 1914-1939*, Routledge, London, 1972.

[13] Clarke's indebtedness to Mannheim was generously expressed in his note, 'Karl Mannheim at the Institute of Education' in F.W. Mitchell, *Sir Fred Clarke, Master-Teacher 1880-1952*, Longman, London, 1967, Appendix B. Clarke persuaded Mannheim, who held a teaching post at LSE, to teach

Institute students during the war. He was appointed to a chair in the sociology of education at the Institute in 1946, dying in 1947.

[14] Academic staff at colleges of education increased from 3334 in 1960 to 11,937 in 1970. The number of students rose from 33,993 in 1961 to 107,386 in 1970. It should be remembered that the traditional two-year course was increased to three years from 1960. Referring to the changed content of study at the colleges, Joan Browne writes, 'Such books as M.V. Daniels: *Activity in the Junior School* and Susan Isaacs' *The Children We Teach*, were replaced or supplemented by *The Study of Education* edited by Professor Tibble and its many offshoots, and by specialist texts on the psychology, sociology and history of education'. See Joan Browne, 'The Transformation of the Education of Teachers in the 1960s' in Edward Fearn and Brian Simon (editors), *Education in the Sixties*, History of Education Society.

[15] Olive Banks surveys recent developments, including the thrust of the new sociology, of neo-Marxism, and their relations to the 'old' (or mainstream) sociology. The extreme divisions of the 1970s, she claims, are being overcome, while the subject itself which displayed 'great vitality' in the 1970s, 'is still very much alive'. See Olive Banks, The Sociology of Education, 1952-1982, *British Journal of Educational Studies*, Volume XXX, Number 1.

[16] Gareth Williams, 'The Economics of Education: Current Debates and Prospects', *British Journal of Educational Studies*, Volume XXX, Number 1. For university studies in administration, See Bone, T.R., 'Educational administration', *British Journal of Educational Studies*, Volume XXX, Number 1.

[17] For the leading papers presented to this enquiry by Paul Hirst, Colin Lacey, Brian Simon and others, see *British Journal of Teacher Education*, Volume 2, Number 1 (1976).

[18] For a pioneering study using anthropological techniques, see Philip Jackson, *Life in Classrooms*, Holt, Rinehart, New York, 1968. Systematic observational studies include the ORACLE publications, e.g. Galton, M., Simon, B., and Croll P., *Inside the Primary Classroom*, Routledge 1980.

The full references for this essay are given in *Studies in Higher Education*, Volume 8, Number 1, 1983.

9: Some Problems of Pedagogy, Revisited*

Twelve years ago I published an article which aimed to highlight the historical neglect of pedagogical studies in England. Entitled 'Why No Pedagogy in England?' this set out to analyse the reasons for this neglect.[1] I argued that these were linked with the traditions, practice and outlook of the dominant schools historically, the 'public' schools, on the one hand, and those of the elementary schools on the other. The public schools placed their major emphasis on character formation rather than on intellectual or cognitive development, a standpoint clearly reflected in their scepticism as regards teacher training (which they rejected). Their objective was to produce leaders for a country with an imperial role. The elementary schools, on the other hand, were primarily concerned with inculcating elementary literacy and numeracy but also with the social-disciplinary role of 'gentling the masses'. The main motivation underlying educational practice in both 'systems', I argued, was more directly concerned with attitude and character formation than with promoting intellectual (or mental) development. And here, I suggested, lies the historical root for the neglect of pedagogy.

This neglect, I argued, was strikingly reflected in the low level of involvement of the country's leading universities (Oxford and Cambridge) in educational (or pedagogical) studies, both historically and more specifically since the 1890s when university education departments began to be established. There has recently been a change here of course, and Oxford now actually has a professor, but this was the most belated appointment of all. As far as the 'public' schools are concerned, it is worth noting the extent to which traditional

---

* Lecture delivered to the Eighth Annual Conference of the Educational Research Network of Northern Ireland, 13 November 1993.

approaches were reinforced on the establishment of the most modern or 'innovative' of these – Gordonstoun in Scotland. This school listed, in its first prospectus (of the mid-1930s), a number of staff members defined as 'character formers'; the actual teachers (of science, maths, literature, etc.) were listed below these. This school, of course, developed as a seminary for princes – first Philip, then Charles and his brothers. It may be said in a sense to have embodied a modern concept of an aristocratic education, but intellectual development was certainly not a leading objective.

I defined the term 'pedagogy' in that essay as the OED did, as 'the science of teaching', and supporting this definition as viable from a book by a leading psychologist/educationist of the late nineteenth century. The author, James Ward, starts by saying that such a science 'must be based on psychology and the cognate sciences'. He goes on:[2]

> To show this we have, indeed, only to consider how the educator works, or rather ought to work, upon a growing mind, *with a definite purpose of attaining an end in view*. For unless it be maintained that systematic observation of the growth of (say) a hundred minds would disclose no uniformities; and unless, further, it can be maintained that for the attainment of a definite end there are no definite means, we must allow. that *if the teacher knows what he wants to do there must be a scientific way of doing it*. Not only so. We must allow not only the possibility of a scientific exposition of the means the educator should employ to attain his end, but we must allow also the possibility of a scientific exposition of the end at which he ought to aim, unless again it be contended that it is impossible by reasoning to make manifest that one form of life and character is preferable to another.

The argument was taken further in that essay. The historic neglect of pedagogy, or 'science of teaching', I suggested, established a kind of vacuum in the area of educational theory applied to teaching. Such theory that was developed and applied, for instance in the first half of this century, having no established criteria for judgement, was highly subject to the winds of fashion – to pedagogical initiatives which 'seemed to work' according to various, sometimes contradictory standards, as also to psychological theories developed elsewhere but now quite arbitrarily applied to education – for instance, Freudianism, psychometry (or mental testing), later Piagetianism. All this, I argued, found its classic expression in the Plowden report of 1967. The theory of child development underlying educational (or teaching) practice encapsulated in that report was, seen in retrospect, an extreme version of what might be called pedagogic, or psychological individualism. The main message was that each child must be seen, and treated, as a unique individual – as a product of initial (or genetic) differences exacerbated in the interactional process from birth to such an extent that the unique character of each individual child is the overriding consideration. The conclusion was that the teacher should ideally monitor each child's development across three parameters, intellectual, emotional and physical, since rates of development differ on each of these. In determining her approach to each individual child, development on each of these three parameters must be taken into account by the teacher.[3]

This was, in effect, a call for the total individualisation of both teaching and learning in the primary classroom (with an average of 35 children per class at that time). No wonder even Plowden characterised the task set the teacher as 'frighteningly high'.[4] Plowden generally defined the teacher's role as to spark, or organise, appropriate activities, to intervene tactfully when necessary, to monitor pupils' development across each of the three parameters, and generally to lead from behind. Group and individualised forms of classroom organisation were encouraged, but particularly the latter. Class teaching sharply *discouraged*.

I argued in my essay that this was a recipe for disaster (although perhaps I did not put it quite so clearly). It was a recipe for disaster because it obviated any possibility of developing effective pedagogic means (or procedures) within the primary classroom. If each child was to be treated individually as unique, how could general pedagogical procedures appropriate for *all* be developed? Yet to achieve the latter lies at the very heart of the concept of pedagogy – the science of teaching. When I wrote that essay, around 1980, I had been involved as co-director with my colleague Maurice Galton, in a five year research programme, known as ORACLE (Observational Research and Classroom Learning Evaluation), concerned precisely to elucidate and analyse classroom processes through long-term systematic observation of a sample of primary classrooms. As a matter of fact I'd been on the job for ten years since ORACLE was based on earlier research projects in which we had honed our techniques. The great majority of the classrooms observed turned out to be unstreamed, so-called 'informal' classrooms; these were situated in three local authority areas near Leicester.

The teachers in our sample in fact overwhelmingly used group and individualised activities across the various areas of the curriculum we observed – to that extent their practice tended to correspond to the Plowden precepts. But so complex was the situation that now developed in the classroom that we found the teachers' managerial skills stretched to the utmost. But here lay a contradiction. In this situation the teachers had neither time nor energy to individualise their interactions with pupils as seen as central by Plowden – that is, to engage in long-term educative dialogues with individual pupils. Their main concern had to be to maintain an ordered and, if you like, a disciplined classroom, allowing movement and talk in moderate quantities but never getting out of hand. The striking result we found was that in such classrooms the teachers were typically highly active, interacting with the pupils for nearly 80 per cent of the time. But the downside of this was the extraordinarily low level of interaction by individual pupils with the same teachers – down to an average of only 2.3 per cent of his or her time (or one minute 23 seconds in a one hour session).[5] This pattern of interaction, we concluded, which we defined as the 'assymetry' of interactional patterns in the classroom, was primarily determined by managerial requirements – where the class's activities were fully individualised (as we found was often the case, even if the pupils sat in groups) interaction with teachers was typically very brief and also, incidentally, primarily didactic. This clearly contradicted the Plowden precepts which, in fact, now appeared as utterly unrealistic.

My essay concluded by arguing that, if we wanted to develop effective pedagogic means relevant to the primary (or for that matter also secondary) classrooms and children we needed to start from the *opposite* premises from those embraced by Plowden. Instead of pin-pointing the supposed needs of each individual child seen as a unique individual, we should start, I argued, by identifying the needs and characteristics of children in general – those common to *all*. If the pedagogic means developed on this basis were found to be inappropriate to particular, individual children (or to groups of children), then of course these would need to be modified, or varied appropriately, based on intensive research. But the main aim and direction of research should be towards evolving pedagogical means relevant to *all* children, at the several stages of mental development (if such stages can be experimentally determined).

This approach, incidentally, would fit naturally into the main tradition of pedagogical thinking and research – from the time of the Jesuits in the sixteenth century, who first sought systematically to develop effective pedagogical means through pooling experience and reflection on trial and error procedures in their schools throughout Europe, and, more recently, through the work of Comenius and his followers on mass education from the seventeenth century onwards. In this tradition can be placed such educational innovators as Robert Owen, Pestalozzi, Herbart – even Froebel and Dewey. It is worth recalling that, although we have lost our way recently, there has been a vibrant tradition of pedagogical research and study in this sense through the centuries, starting from the premises I have defined; that is, searching out that which is common. Probably the most recent school of psychologically informed pedagogy in this sense, is that linked with the name of Lev Vigotski and his talented followers (Luria, Leontiev and others) in the recently defunct Soviet Union, and indeed the world-wide interest and involvement now in pursuing research of this character in Europe (especially Spain and Scandinavia) and the United States is noteworthy.

I apologise for this lengthy introductory passage, but I wanted to set the scene for a re-think of these ideas now, in the mid-1990s, twelve years after the publication of that essay. For much has happened to transform the educational scene and a re-think in the light of the new situation may have value. I hasten to say that I hold no brief for many of the changes that have been made – particularly the structural changes brought about by the 1988 Act and more recently by the 1993 Act. That goes for the whole policy of opting out and the irresponsible attack on local education authorities in England and Wales which has taken a whole number of forms, and especially the introduction of market force mechanisms within the school system generally leading to increased differentiation and hierarchisation of school systems serving local communities – the league table initiative is of course part of all this. But this is not the place to develop that particular critique. One aspect of the current 'reforms' does, however, hold promise for the future if its development can be effectively guided by educationists – those who *understand*. I refer to the national curriculum, though not to its testing adjunct.

This, I know, is a very controversial issue among teachers and educationists generally. But, however hurriedly introduced in the 1988 Act – without any consultation whatever, relying instead on the bureaucratic subject-based objectives pattern largely rejected by

151

curriculum experts (eg Lawrence Stenhouse); and however subject it has been to unacceptable politically based short-term initiatives and revisions, the fact is that a national curriculum has been put in place and, if there is anything in democratic procedures, that curriculum can be modified through the expression of public opinion, as indeed we are to some extent seeing now with the acceptance recently of the main theses of Sir Ron Dearing's interim report (and, later, of his final report). The intense and unreasonable pressure the national curriculum and testing has put on teachers has been made very clear by the actions of the various teacher unions in 1993 – this unceasing pressure, of course, deflects teachers from their real job of educating their pupils and so of developing through their own practice appropriate pedagogical means in the sense used in this essay.

But it is worth recalling at this point that the idea of a common curriculum within the restructured comprehensive schools of England, Wales and Scotland goes back to the very inception of these schools. This was an objective shared by the pioneers of comprehensive education, particularly by their more advanced teachers who were determined to prove in practice that children who had previously been divided into grammar and modern schools *could* be educated together, and study the same subjects, within the new-style comprehensive schools. In 1957, nearly forty years ago, we published *New Trends in English Education* in which a number of teachers specifically argued in favour of a common course within the new-type comprehensive schools, and some advanced schools actually put this into practice, so far as it was then possible, given the divided examination structure of those days which militated in favour of dividing pupils into three groups, bands or streams from the age of 12 or 13, one aiming at GCE, one (after 1972) at CSE and a third at *no* examination. At roughly the same time (that is, in the 1960s) the swing to non-streaming in the primary school, as a deliberate policy determined by teachers, took off with extraordinary rapidity and put an end to rigid curriculum differentiation within primary schools in England, Wales and Scotland as a whole. True, individualisation, supported ideologically by Piagetian ideas, was now substituted in the primary schools as we have seen; but less so in the secondary schools.

Nor should we forget the long battle that took place, led by teachers, for the GCSE – the substitution of a single exam at sixteen for the GCE/CSE divide. This was finally conceded by Keith Joseph in 1984 after the earlier Labour government (under Shirley Williams as

Secretary of State) had funked the issue, losing it in a welter of 'discussion'. Much could be said about all this, but that's another story. The fact is that the idea of a common curriculum, however defined, was a standard born by advanced, progressive teachers determined to develop a real and effective unity within comprehensive schools now, in England, Wales and Scotland, comprising the vast majority of state maintained schools. I realise the situation differed in Northern Ireland, but no doubt similar pressures developed there also, though taking a different form.

This pressure, or move towards unification both at the primary and the secondary stage was a process which developed its power first in the 1970s and then, later, in the early and mid-1980s. The 1988 Act, accepting the reality of the move towards a common curriculum, but insisting on top-down control, brought in the so-called national curriculum, seen by many as defining an entitlement curriculum for all. This can be interpreted, then, as embodying a positive potential. And in these days we need, I suggest, to grasp and reinforce whatever seems positive in order to strengthen a vision of what might be when better times come, as surely they must.

I want to argue that acceptance of a national curriculum, whatever its current weaknesses and contradictions, creates a new situation in that it attempts to define common objectives for *all* pupils across the main subjects including English, Maths and Science, both in the field of primary and secondary education (to sixteen). And, if you remember, this is what I defined as the *first necessary condition* for identifying effective pedagogic means. This represents a profound shift from Plowden objectives and procedures which in essence denied the viability of the promotion of such common objectives.

Now perhaps I can attempt to concretise what I have in mind by a critical look at three crucial documents relevant to my thesis, and to primary education in particular – the Alexander report ('Three Wise Men') and two responses to it, that by the National Curriculum Council and that by OFSTED.[6] The Alexander report was, of course, produced in almost impossible, politically motivated and determined conditions, as part of Kenneth Clarke's sudden onslaught on primary education when Secretary of State. This gives it more significance, perhaps, as part of the history of the battle for position within the Tory party leadership than for education – in that Clarke was overtly using his position as Secretary of State to strengthen his support among the Tory Right wing (to whom he was suspect). Nevertheless I think

Robin Alexander, Jim Rose and Chris Woodhead were right to undertake the task set, and to accept the challenge. It was an opportunity to open up a debate on primary education generally. Alexander, to whom most of the content of the report is rightly attributed, was chosen to undertake this enquiry on the grounds of his long-term, detailed analysis of primary policy and procedures at Leeds, a job willingly undertaken for the Leeds education authority. This earlier report, based on in-depth research including much classroom observation, was both critical (of school and classroom procedures) and supportive. As a result of this experience, and his own books and writings on primary education, Robin Alexander has certainly established a considerable reputation in this field, both as a critic and supporter of new approaches. His critique has, on the whole, been well received by teachers and others.

Alexander's report, though covering a wide area, hurriedly completed, and written with economy, does raise pedagogic issues in the sense I am discussing these, and to my knowledge, is one of the first public documents to do so. He draws attention to weaknesses inherent in present practice very much on the lines that I did earlier, and indeed the ORACLE research programme and its findings is one of the sources he acknowledges as influencing his approach. He points out the essential similarity in the research findings of other projects which, since ORACLE, have taken further the in-depth analysis of primary practice – particularly Peter Mortimore and his team's intensive effective schools project completed for the ILEA, and others.[7] From these sources, and his own long-term Leeds project, he (and the other authors) reach a major conclusion that I believe to be important. This is that primary classroom practice, based loosely on Plowden, creates an 'excessively complex' classroom management situation which presents, overall, an almost impossible task to the teacher. Exaggerated individualism as I argued earlier, presents the main problem. Perhaps I may quote from a single paragraph which reflects my thesis rather closely. 'Teachers need to reject', the authors say, 'the essentially unrealistic belief that pupils' individual differences provide the central clue as to how the simultaneous teaching of many individuals can be organised. The goals of primary education', they go on 'are common to all pupils. It is from this reality that planning for teaching should start'.[8]

The report's recommendations, to the evident chagrin of our political masters, totally rejected radical solutions such as the re-introduction of streaming, even if there was endorsement of ability grouping within the normal unstreamed class. There is also an emphasis on the re-introduction of whole class teaching and, of course, many proposals relating to the national curriculum, the need for specialist and/or semi-specialist teachers, and so on – even if the report does strongly emphasise the need for a revision of the national curriculum as being over-powering in its demands it tends to accept its behests as the Tables of the Law. But maybe this was seen as a political necessity. There are emphases in the report also on what I would call a Vigotskian approach which is positive, even if the implications are not effectively elaborated. But if I were to be critical, I would say the chance was missed for raising as a crucial issue for discussion the need for a much more detailed elaboration of actual pedagogical requirements in primary teaching. That issue (as with Plowden) is fudged.

Alexander focuses on classroom organisation – that is true, correct and important. He focuses also on the teacher's need to develop specific, and neglected, teaching skills – for instance those of explanation, questioning and so on. Attention is also devoted to classroom organisation, the choice of group, individual and whole class teaching, and the need to reflect on all this and for teachers to adopt *what seems to them* the best, or most productive or appropriate strategies or tactics. Though a number of pedagogical issues are raised here, this is as far as it goes. He does not enter into the question as to how pedagogical means, designed to facilitate mental, or cognitive, development of *all* children are to be elaborated, nor what implications these might have for classroom organisation and teaching techniques; and yet it is this issue which lies at the heart of the matter. Maybe it would be asking too much that he should tangle with these questions, and his two colleagues, a Chief HMI (albeit with much successful primary practice to his credit as a headmaster) and the chief executive of the now defunct National Curriculum Council, could hardly, perhaps, be expected to chance their arms in this field. So this crucial issue concerning identification of appropriate pedagogical means, which surely should underlie classroom organisation *and* the practice of teaching, is left aside. And that marginalisation, I suggest, is very much in the English tradition. Why no Pedagogy in England? remains a relevant question. That said, attention should be drawn to Alexander's emphasis on the need to pose an appropriate intellectual challenge to children. 'Good teaching does not merely keep step with the pupils but challenges and stretches their thinking' (para 128). Learning tasks should be provided which not only engage the pupil's current level of understanding but also provide the challenge 'which will move that understanding forward' (para 137). These ideas are close to Vigotski's and provide a base for new thinking and a more positive practice.

The Alexander report, as is well known, formed the basis for the assessment and recommendations relating to primary education presented to the Secretary of State in the two reports which shortly followed – that by the National Curriculum Council and by OFSTED. But it would be naive to expect much from either of these. Once again these were produced, or published, in a blaze of highly politicised press conferences, the process involving leaks, early press releases and so on by the then very publicity conscious Secretary of State (still Kenneth Clarke). Deliberate attempts were made, with the aid of so-called 'education correspondents' of the tabloid press (*Daily Mail, Sun*) to claim that both reports recommended a return to streaming (see pp175-79). In fact neither did. Both turned out to be relatively bland documents, no doubt drafted by civil servants, recommending steps to ease the introduction of a perhaps modified national curriculum and testing model. Apart from some references to the teacher's role in determining classroom organisation, a bow in the direction of whole class and specialist teaching, neither of these documents contributed so much as one word relevant to our current concerns – pedagogy. This also, of course, was directly in the English, dare I say Philistine, tradition.

I turn now to the heart of the matter. Can I elaborate what I mean by pedagogy – or adopting a pedagogically determined approach to teaching and learning appropriate to the objectives defined in an agreed, perhaps a national curriculum? As I understand it, Vigotski focussed attention on the deliberate formation of specific elementary concepts – say of number – in young children, then of groups, or sets, of related concepts, and finally of higher order mental operations underlying human skills or abilities. Such mental abilities, and their related thought processes in his view can and should be deliberately formed in the process of education through the careful structuring of the child's activity under adult guidance. What the child can do with the aid of an adult today, he stated, he will be able to do independently tomorrow (a statement frequently repeated to me by Vigotski's distinguished co-worker and friend, Alexander Luria). This is the significance of Vigotski's Zone of Potential Development – that zone which lies between a child's current, or existing level of achievement (as shown, for instance, by a test), and that same child's actual achievement *with adult help*. That area Vigotski defined as a zone of *potential* development, where rapid advances could potentially be made by the child. Teaching, therefore, should not be based on assessment of the child's *current* level. It should be directed beyond that, to exploit the zone of *potential* development. Pedagogy, according to Vigotski, must be 'oriented not towards the yesterdays of development but towards its tomorrow'. 'The only good teaching', he goes on, 'is that which outpaces development'.[9] These ideas, incidentally, were taken up and developed in his own way by Jerome Bruner who threw his weight 20 or more years ago in a consistent effort to persuade psychologists in the United States to use their expertise to assist the development of effective pedagogical means.

The psychologist's particular contribution, said Bruner in *The Relevance of Education* (1972), is 'to convert skills and knowledge to forms and exercises that fit growing minds'; the pedagogical problem is 'how to represent knowledge, how to sequence it, how to embody it in a form appropriate to young learners'. How one manages to time the steps in pedagogy to match unfolding capacities, how one manages to instruct without making the learner dependent, and how one manages to do both these while keeping 'alive zest for further learning – these', writes Bruner, are very complicated questions that do not yield easy answers. It is from this analysis that, in an earlier essay (1964) entitled 'The Perfectibility of Intellect', Bruner stated his view – that for any knowledge or 'empowering skill' in society there is a corresponding form that is within the grasp of a young learner at the stage of development 'where one finds him' – concluding 'that any subject can be taught to anybody at any age in some form that is both interesting and honest'.[10]

I believe that Bruner may have retracted that latter, very challenging statement, but that is by the way. The point that is relevant to our discussion, and worth drawing attention to, is Bruner's argument that it is the job of psychologists to identify these means and to provide this assistance to practising educators. One of the essays in the book mentioned (1972) comprises Bruner's attempt to persuade American psychologists to concern themselves with this pressing problem – 'I hoped to persuade them', he writes, 'that developmental psychology without a theory of pedagogy was as empty an enterprise as a theory of pedagogy that ignored the nature of growth'.[11] In Britain, it seems to me, few psychologists proper (ie in University departments) concern themselves in any serious way with pedagogical questions – or with education – either 20 years ago when Bruner wrote that appeal, or now. So Bruner's plea is as relevant here as in the United States. For Bruner, it is clear, the elaboration of effective pedagogic means is *the* key to an effective education. Further, education, he held, can be a powerful cultural influence. Educational experiences can be ordered and structured to enable people more fully to realise their humanity and bring about social change, so creating a world according to their felt and recognised objectives. 'Man is not a naked ape,' he wrote in this connection, 'but a culture-clothed human being, hopelessly ineffective without the prosthesis provided by culture.[12]

The Vigotskian approach, taken up and developed in his own way by Bruner, was developed, it is highly relevant to note, in and as a critique of Piagetianism, at least in its early form. His concept of the need to mount a consistent challenge to the child to reach higher levels, to attack the next stage in any intellectual endeavour was articulated partly in criticism of Piaget's theory of stages and, in particular, of the Piagetian theory of 'readiness' which, unfortunately for us, won hands down the battle for the minds of teacher educators in England after the unregretted demise of psychometry in the late 1950s and early 1960s. Psychometry set out to show that a child's learning was determined by genetic endowment and that this was all there was to be said about it. Its hegemony, which lasted for decades, resulted in the marginalisation of any research or even thinking about *human learning* – witness the remarks of the psychologists invited to contribute to Nuffield curriculum reform projects in the 60s. At a meeting convened in 1962 to discuss possible research on the intellectual development of children in areas relevant to the curriculum projects (physics and chemistry), leading psychologists held that little advice was possible since 'so little research had, as yet, been undertaken with British children'.[13] Piagetianism at least accepted a dynamic view of child development, and of learning, but constricted it within an iron determinism through the theory of stages. If we need a theoretical foundation for a theory of learning which can be helpful in existing circumstances, then I suggest we need to look to Vigotski, Luria and their school for its foundations.

In this country there has been so little interest in all this that there are very few who know what has been achieved through the work of Vigotski and his followers. Little has been translated. Thirty years ago my wife and I published a whole set of research papers translated from the Russian bearing on this entire issue, giving pride of place to Vigotski's article of 1934 from which I quoted earlier. Other articles dealt with children's learning in mathematics, language, science and other subjects, utilised research techniques unknown then or since in Britain and shed a flood of light on the conditions affecting children's mental development.[14] Margaret Donaldson and others have done similar work in Britain, but it has not yet been taken into the mainstream[15]. I believe we can gain greatly by excavating this tradition and applying it, together with related work by Bruner and others, to our situation here – for the first time the conditions are ripe for just such an infusion of new ideas – or ideas which, though now quite old, have never been taken up in any serious way in Britain.

All this, of course, has important implications not only for teacher training and education but also for universities, colleges and teachers in terms of the promotion of research and development needed to underpin, lend substance to, and so promote a truly pedagogical approach to school learning. And here we confront current initiatives by the present government. Let us focus first on teacher education.

It is widely recognised that the early years are quite crucial for children's mental, or cognitive development. Indeed it is hardly necessary to argue the point. In terms of linguistic development, that of number – numeracy generally – and, crucially, of the formation of early scientific concepts, the years between four and 9 or 10 are central. Indeed it is at this phase that teaching and learning, based on sound pedagogical principles, are probably most rewarding. Teachers for this phase, then, need to be true professionals, *au fait* with both the theoretical foundations underlying practice, and the necessary teaching skills to create the situations best adapted to ensuring the formation of relevant concepts, so promoting children's mental development, their abilities and skills.

There can be nothing to be said, then, in favour of the government's recent proposal to recruit a class of so-called teachers for a one-year course to be responsible for teaching children up to Key Stage 1 (to seven plus). Such a proposal could emanate only from people who have *no conception*, and I mean that literally, of what is even now required of teachers of children of that age. As a result of intense and widespread opposition, this proposal was dropped – but that it could be made at all provides a searing insight into the nature of government thinking on this issue.

The new (November 1993) Education Bill covering teacher education, establishing yet another unelected and unaccountable quango, the Teacher Training Agency, threatens in various ways both the quality of teacher education generally and the involvement of universities in research and development in this whole area. It is too early yet to predict outcomes, but, if the measures proposed are carried through the opportunity now existing to make something of a break-through in developing effective pedagogic means will be lost. Instead we need now to mount a systematic attack on the pedagogical issues underlying the new dispensation. New-type, multi-disciplinary research teams involving experienced teachers (especially those research orientated), subject specialists, psychologists (especially those interested in learning theory) and similar like-minded innovative people, covering the main subjects (or 'areas of experience' if that approach is favoured) could be given the task of cracking the problems involved. It is necessary to establish both a curriculum – a sequence or sequential series of issues/problems – *and* to determine, through experiment, appropriate pedagogical means. Since children's learning requires activity on their part, sets of structured activities, related to each other, need careful and precise definition. This applies to all fields – mathematics, science, language, environmental studies, technology, even geography and history. If I seem to emphasise the need for precision, this is because it is this which has been lacking. And it is this which is the condition for a later flexibility of approach.

Perhaps we will have to wait for better times before a full and clear programme of advance can be formulated, and carried through. In the meantime it is important to clarify objectives. The green shoots of a new pedagogically viable approach to teaching are appearing. They need to be but watered, as Yeats once wrote, to spread on every side.

Notes

[1] Brian Simon, 'Why No Pedagogy in England?', in Brian Simon and William Taylor, eds., *Education in the Eighties, the Central Issues* (London 1981), reprinted in Brian Simon, *Does Education Matter?* (London 1985), and in Roger Dale, Ross Fergusson and Alison Robertson of the Open University, *Frameworks for Teaching* (London 1988).
[2] J. Ward, *Psychology Applied to Education* (Cambridge 1926), p1 (my italics, BS). Though published in 1926, Ward's lecture from which this excerpt is taken was delivered in 1879.
[3] The Plowden Report, *Children and their Primary Schools* (London 1967), Vol 1, paras 75 and 875.

[4] *Ibid.*

[5] Maurice Galton, Brian Simon and Paul Croll, *Inside the Primary Classroom* (London 1980), p60-3.

[6] Robin Alexander, Jim Rose, Chris Woodhead, *Curriculum Organisation and Classroom Practice in Primary Schools, a discussion paper* (DES, nd, 1992); National Curriculum Council, *The National Curriculum at Key Stages 1 and 2* (National Curriculum Council, January 1993); Office for Standards in Education (OFSTED), *Curriculum Organisation and Classroom Practice in Primary Schools, a follow-up report* (OFSTED 1993).

[7] Mortimore P, Sammons P, Stoll L, Lewis D, Ecob R, *School Matters: the Junior Years* (Open Books 1988).

[8] Alexander, Rose, Woodhead, *op.cit.*, paras 118, 106.

[9] LS Vigotski, 'Learning and Mental Development at School Age', in Brian and Joan Simon, eds., *Educational Psychology in the USSR*, (London 1963), pp21-34. This now famous article was written in 1934, the year of the author's death, aged 38.

[10] Jerome Bruner, *The Relevance of Education* (London 1972), pp66, 55, 122, 18.

[11] *Ibid.*, pxiv

[12] *Ibid.*, p131. For a fascinating, and highly relevant discussion of both Piaget's and Vigotski's contribution to education, see Jerome Bruner's intellectual autobiography, *In Search of Mind* (London and New York, 1983), pp136-46.

[13] See M. Waring, *Social Pressures and Curriculum Innovation*, (London 1979), p133.

[14] Brian and Joan Simon, eds., *Educational Psychology in the USSR* (London 1963). This had been preceded by Brian Simon (ed.), *Psychology in the Soviet Union* (London 1957).

[15] Margaret Donaldson, *A Study of Children's Thinking* (London, 1963; *Children's Minds* (London, 1978). Attention may be drawn to Sara Meadows' recently published *The Child as Thinker*, subtitled 'The Development and Acquisition of Cognition in Childhood' (Routledge, 1993). This presents Vigotski's outlook (and that of 'neo-Vigotskians') effectively, bringing out its basic differences from Piagetian approaches. This book reflects a welcome new interest in Vigotski's work among psychologists though its pedagogic implications are hardly elaborated.

10: The Politics of Comprehensive Education: a Retrospective Analysis*

Comprehensive schools can claim a rather special distinction. No other type of institution in the history of English education has aroused such opposition, or, if you like, controversy. While there was certainly disagreement, particularly among rival religious sects, relating to the establishment of elementary schools, generally speaking by 1870 there was a widespread consensus that such a form of schooling was both necessary and desirable. Grammar schools, under the 1902 Act, proved popular and there was certainly no strong campaign against their establishment, though the Labour movement opposed their elitist character. Technical schools, the later senior elementary schools, then secondary modern – all these had a relatively easy birth and development, at least in the early stages, as also did special schools for the so-called educationally subnormal and, in a different category, universities, technical colleges, colleges of art and of further education – later even the polytechnics. No great campaigns were levelled against any of these. In our time this fate has been reserved for only one type of educational institution, the comprehensive secondary school, and the campaign still continues, rising to a crescendo recently – the Prime

* Lecture delivered to the History of Education Society, May 1992.

Minister himself participating, and even leading the pack. The Education Reform Act, it could be argued, had one major target and one only: the comprehensive secondary school.

Why is this? What are we tangling with here? Why has the comprehensive school specifically become so battered a political football? Why is it appropriate today to talk about 'The Politics of' comprehensive reorganization?

I recently completed a lengthy review of Neil Smelser's interesting study entitled *Social Paralysis and Social Change*, subtitled *British Working Class Education in the 19th Century* (1991). The title is unusual but has clear implications. A sociologist turned historian, hailing from the USA, Smelser is able to evaluate British developments and social processes with what one might call an uncluttered eye. He draws attention at the start to what he defines as certain leading 'primordial characteristics' of Britain which need to be understood to interpret the paralysis that affected social policy in education in the nineteenth century. These are, first, the extraordinary power of the imagery of social hierarchy, historically rooted in the monarchy, the feudal tradition, the peerage, gentry and so on and, following from this, the centrality of class expressed in the principle of segregation in education on class lines. 'For each class of society' (Smelser quotes Kay Shuttleworth), 'there is an appropriate education', (Smelser, p45). Third, the centrality of religion – and especially of the Church of England as by law established; and fourth, the force or power of what he calls regionalism, with special reference to Ireland, Wales and Scotland (we might note here that opposition to comprehensive education is far more specific to England than to Wales or Scotland). These primordial features relate, in Smelser's analysis, to the nineteenth century, during which there was a shift from oligarchic forms of government to democratic. That latter process continues (or does it?), but so, also, perhaps, do the power and influence of Smelser's primordial characteristics.

An overarching analysis like this may have more validity than at first seems apparent. It helps to explain, perhaps, the particular role of the grammar school historically – an institution directly threatened by comprehensive reorganization. Grammar schools, if we think of their endowed variety, have long-established links with the aristocracy, the gentry, the upper classes generally. One has only to look at the names of those who were governors of the local grammar schools in, say, Leicestershire in the nineteenth century to see this. These schools, and those established after 1902, also had close links, through the endowed school system, with the top public or 'Great' schools where the aristocracy increasingly educated their own offspring. They had links, however tenuous, with the monarchy – when Brockington. Leicestershire's long-living and distinguished director of education from 1902 to 1947, named the revived or new grammar schools in the county after 1902 he christened them King Edward VII schools, so getting into hot water with Winston Churchill, Home Secretary, for arrogating this title without consultation, as he once told me after retirement. These schools also had links with the Church – indeed were often held, in law, to be Anglican. Finally, grammar schools were very much an English phenomenon – Scottish and Welsh developments differed. So these schools specifically embodied, or had links with all four of Smelser's primordial features. To disturb them would be like a rape.

There was, of course, a different tradition – that embodied in John Brinsley's concept of the grammar school as 'the common country school', as also in those schools established and controlled by often embryonic forms of local government and, of course, by town councils or boroughs; it is the historian's task to reveal this tradition and evaluate its importance and historical significance. Much of that work, however, still remains to be done.[1]

But the fact is that comprehensive education threatened the grammar school or its existence as a discrete entity. It was bound to – by its very *raison d'être*. In 1960 there were about 1300 grammar schools in England and Wales and only 130 comprehensives. In 1990, 30 years later, there were 150 grammar schools and well over 3000 comprehensives. These figures dramatically point to the rate and extent of change. The shock waves generated by the growth of comprehensive schools, I suggest, may have had a wider resonance than simply on those directly affected (who may indeed have benefited); it excited atavistic memories, images and reactions perhaps much more widely, appearing to threaten all that was traditional and stable in our society: the Royal family (image of stability?), the Church establishment, hierarchical relations generally which, many believe, underlie social stability. I suggest that Margaret Thatcher was well aware of this when she appealed to popular sentiment, rather than supporting the rationalizing activities of Tory shire counties and other local authorities, in exempting specific prestigious grammar schools from comprehensive reorganization plans in the early 1970s. She was appealing to these atavistic memories still capable of evoking a wider resonance among those sections of the population to whom she directed her appeal.

Possibly all this was not sufficiently taken into account by those pioneering the movement. Faced with such a *bouleversement*, one thing that was certainly necessary was clarity of purpose, unwavering determination and above all political will. Part of our problem, I suggest, is that, although these qualities were certainly shown by many, the movement generally fell short of requirements on all these counts.

I should like now to pick up how the comprehensive (originally 'multilateral') school first entered the politics of education in this country – at least on the national stage. It will be recalled that the Spens Committee grappled with the problem. This committee was concerned with the future pattern of secondary education 'with special reference to technical schools'. It received a good deal of 'evidence' supporting the idea of the single secondary school (or something akin) – from several teacher organizations, those representing the Labour movement and from local government associations.[2] So powerful was this evidence that in fact the committee, when it reported, devoted much of the introduction to the whole report in setting the argument aside. The report finally, as published on 30 December 1938, as is very well known indeed, came down firmly for the tripartite solution, while allowing that multilateral schools might be the right solution in sparsely populated rural areas and new housing estates. My mother (Shena D. Simon), incidentally, was an active member of this committee, and she changed her mind quite soon. But, generally speaking, the historical importance of the Spens report lies in its powerful support for the tripartite system – after all, the coming into being of technical schools became actually part of the committee's brief.

By this time, 1938 – or, more precisely, 1939 – no political party had embraced the concept of the single school, but this was now to change. In December 1937 the Executive Committee (EC) of the Labour Party, realizing that a general election was coming up (it would have had to be held by June 1940), decided to clarify policy across a whole range of areas including education, health, the rating system, town and country planning and other matters. To carry this out the committee established six new advisory committees of which the Education Advisory Committee was one.[3] The job was to work out a 'comprehensive statement on education policy'. Twenty-five members were appointed. These included first, as Chairman (as they were then called), Morgan Jones MP. He had been Parliamentary Secretary to the Board of Education both in the 1924 Labour (minority) government, and again in 1929-31 and was, therefore, the senior 'educationist' in the party. Membership comprised several MPs and some others. Among these appointed were J. Chuter Ede (Parliamentary Secretary during the Second World War), Michael Stewart (Secretary of State briefly but importantly in 1964-5), George Tomlinson (Minister of Education 1947-51), H.B. Lees Smith MP, the once fiery W.G. Cove, another MP. Reginald Sorenson MP, R.H. Tawney (a very conscientious attender), the very competent and committed Barbara Drake (much involved in the London County Council and its plans for multilateral schools – a niece of Beatrice Webb's), Elsie Parker, a lively NUT President about this time, W.H. Spikes, teacher and outstanding propagandist for the comprehensive school (leading member of the NUT), Lionel Elvin, (later Principal of Ruskin College and Director of the London Institute of Education), two representatives of the National Association of Labour Teachers, and myself, 'Assistant Secretary' to Barbara Drake, minute taker and producer, and general dogsbody. Don't ask me how I came to be doing this job, but I was invited to be a member from the start. Morgan Jones, the chairman, died early in 1939, being succeeded by the loveable George Tomlinson, with Chuter Ede in reserve when he couldn't attend. Ellen Wilkinson, it is worth noting, was not a member of this committee and attended no meetings.

This committee was active across quite a wide range of policy issues. Here there is only time to focus on one of these – the multilateral school. On 13 February 1939, just six weeks after its publication, the committee discussed a lengthy memo on the Spens Report, drafted by Barbara Drake. In succeeding drafts we can see the policy-making process in action. This first draft concluded by coming down in favour of recommending to the Labour Party's EC that it adopt the concept of multilateral schools as policy, but how were they to be introduced? The original draft puts the issue like this:

Noone suggests that a general system of multilateral schools could be established at once. Nor is it desirable at any time that all schools should conform to exactly the same type, but each should be encouraged to develop a special character and individuality of its own. There is, on the other hand, a strong case to be made for a general development of 'multilateral' schools as the goal of long term policy

On my copy of this draft emendations are made in pencil here, reflecting agreements for modification after discussion (presumably). The pencilled amendments give the following reading for the final sentence:

> There is, on the other hand, a strong case to be made for an immediate policy on development of 'multilateral' schools.

So there was a sharpening of the formulation: instead of being 'the goal of a long term policy', there should be 'an immediate policy' for their development. However, after this preliminary discussion the draft document was extensively reformulated. When it returned to the committee a month later the final sentence was greatly toughened. It now read:

> The time has now come when local education authorities should be required to plan a systematic development of 'multilateral' schools as an immediate practical policy.

So there was a three-stage process of formulation. An original draft, discussion of this and reformulation, resulting in what was in fact a pretty tough statement involving (although it may not have been recognized at the time) specific legislation on this issue. That issue, the means by which this policy was to be implemented, remained a hot one for the next 40 years (or more?).

Now this was the policy proposed by the advisory committee, and so far as I know accepted by the Executive Committee. In 1942 this was given expression, if in a modified guise, at the Labour Party conference where a resolution called on the Board of Education 'to encourage, as a general policy, the development of a new type of multilateral school'. We know the policy, although on the books as it were, was not implemented either by Ellen Wilkinson or by George Tomlinson during the post-war Labour administrations. And here we see the first example of the lack of political will to implement the policy, without which nothing could be achieved.

It is certainly arguable that the post-war Labour government did have the opportunity to introduce comprehensive education. Other countries in fact took this road at that time, pre-eminently Sweden of course, but also, under American tutelage, Japan. This issue has been much discussed, and I am not going to argue it here – either way.[4] But that there was a missed opportunity I think there is no doubt. At the very least the labour government need not so ruthlessly have actually *imposed* the tripartite solution (which later, with much agony, had to be undone).

However, let us take the whole matter further in time – to the mid-1950s and up to the issue of Circular 10/65 which, you may remember, did not 'require' local authorities to submit plans for comprehensive education (as proposed by the Education Advisory Committee) but *requested* them to do so: Let us briefly trace the decision-making process. Here I must acknowledge assistance from Norman Morris, fellow historian of education and, unusually, one who played an important part in this process within the Labour Party.

Passing over the bleak post-war period, which, as we know, saw several sharp confrontations between the Labour Party conference and its decisions and actual government policy on this precise issue, we arrive at 1952-3 – years when the Labour Party conferences finally insisted that, as Norman Morris has put it to me, 'comprehensive education was now firmly on the agenda for action by a Labour government'. The 1952 conference confirmed comprehensive education as party policy. At the 1953 conference a new draft policy statement *Challenge to Britain* was up for discussion. This proposed a nationally imposed two-tier system of comprehensive education. This was not popular either in the party, or among its educational spokespersons. A key amendment was actually proposed at the conference by Norman Morris and seconded by Muriel Forbes. Instead of the system proposed in the draft statement, the amendment proposed that local authorities, on being *required* to submit a reorganization plan to eliminate selection at eleven, would themselves propose how this would be implemented in their areas. This amendment received overwhelming support. We should note that the formulation included the key word 'required'. As I suggested earlier, this would actually involve legislation; but it seems that this may not have been fully recognized at this time. It does indicate, however, that the political will to make the change was now once more in the ascendant.

Summing this up, as Norman Morris does in an unpublished memo on this issue, at the 1953 conference the Party agreed that 'it was for the government to lay down the principles of reorganization, but implementation should be left to each local authority'. Five years later, at the 1958 conference, this policy was repeated and strengthened. In a new policy statement, *Learning to Live*, written by Michael Stewart, it is argued that it would be for local authorities to carry through the planning and the implementation of comprehensive education in their localities. A future Labour government, according to this (1958) policy statement would, therefore, *require* local authorities to prepare and submit their own plans. Final sanction would require ministerial approval.

Conference returned to this again, and at a crucial moment: that is, in 1963. The resolution there is vaguely formulated (and, I suspect, lacked the guiding hand of our colleague), but the intention is now clear. A composite resolution on education was on the agenda, the relevant section of which pledges the Labour Party 'to set up a universal system of comprehensive education and to abolish the 11 plus' by 'converting permissive into compulsory legislation'. This is an odd, imprecise formulation, incidentally, but the need for legislation was apparently here overtly recognized – I think, for the first time.

Well, the Labour Party did win the 1964 election and formed a government, with a majority of three only, but still – the ball was at their feet. What happened?

We may have to wait till 1995 to find out precisely, but we can reconstruct events. In practice the outcome was that the government decided to jettison the long-standing policy of 'requiring' local authorities to produce plans and, instead, to produce a circular substituting (if you like) the word 'request'. One outcome of this decision may be that we still do not have universal comprehensive education in England a generation (27 years) later.

The essence of the matter is succinctly expressed by Edward Short in his book *Whip to Wilson* (1989):

> On 21 January (1965) there was to be a full-scale debate in the Commons on comprehensive education. On the previous Tuesday, the Cabinet considered a proposal by Michael Stewart ... that he should announce legislation requiring recalcitrant local education authorities to end selection at eleven. In spite of a lucid explanation by Michael, the cabinet rejected his plea and decided that the case for comprehensive schools should be put to the local authorities in a carefully drafted circular which asked for their cooperation. After an appropriate period of, say, a year, we would be able to judge how far we could move

169

without legislation. But our manifesto had said 'secondary education will be reorganised on comprehensive lines'.

And so a third dream receded in almost as many weeks – transport, Crown Lands Commission, comprehensive education. I was extremely apprehensive about the effect of these retreats from the manifesto on our backbenchers and on the Labour party outside Parliament; for their support and enthusiasm alone could sustain us in office.

Later, Short says, talking of Crosland's period of office:

In spite of all the efforts of Tony Crosland and his successors, of which I was one, the government's refusal to legislate and the Chancellor's refusal to make funds available meant that comprehensive reorganisation was often a botched up job from the start.

It seems that the villain of the piece, in the Cabinet, may have been Dick Crossman, allied perhaps with George Wigg and Harold Wilson, though Michael Stewart, in his biography, rebuts Crossman's interpretation (in his *Diaries*) of Cabinet discussions on this issue as, in some respects, 'pure invention'. His own account is not, however, by any means altogether clear.[5] I had intended to approach Michael Stewart for a talk about all this some time ago, but unfortunately, just as I began to make arrangements, he became seriously ill and shortly after died. That source has gone for ever. There is a lesson here for oral historians.

The story of the January events of 1965, I fear, is hardly an heroic one. But let us just follow it through to complete the record.

Towards the end of the 1960s, under mounting pressure from its own constituency (teachers, party branches, etc.), the Labour government finally decided to take action. Ted Short is now Secretary of State. He produces his own (short) Bill, much criticized. Nevertheless its general effect, had it passed into law, would have been to impose the duty of submitting non-selective plans on all LEAs in England and Wales. This had its second reading in February 1970, but fell victim to Wilson's decision to go to the country in June that year.

The rest can be shortly told. Almost *the first act* (note!) of the Heath government, now with an abrasive Secretary of State, was to withdraw Circular 10/65. Actually Mrs Thatcher found, on taking office in June 1970, that you cannot 'withdraw' a circular. What you can do, however, is to issue another one, saying the opposite (or whatever). So already on 30 June (1970), just three weeks after Parliament reassembled, Circular 10/70 was published. This stated that, in future, there was to be no uniform pattern imposed centrally. Local authorities were to be given back their 'autonomy', and it was up to them to propose whatever systems, or better alterations to individual schools, they liked.

As we now know, this attempt to hold back what had become, in Thatcher's own words, a 'roller coaster' had only limited success, though it certainly had some. But when Labour returned in 1974 it took them *over a year even to begin to take action*, in spite of the precedent of Short's abortive Bill of 1970. Fred Mulley, the 'forgotten' Minister, tabled a Bill in 1975 'requiring' (shades of Labour's EAC of forty years earlier) local authorities to go comprehensive – or, rather, empowering the Secretary of State 'to call for proposals to complete reorganization'.[6] This received Royal Assent on 22 November 1976, and was indeed followed (unusually) by action by the new Secretary of State, Shirley Williams, almost immediately thereafter.

However, that government had a difficult time and did not have long to run. In May 1979 the Conservatives were back. They presented two Bills on education in their first six months. Already in the debate on the Queen's speech Carlisle had announced that the government 'will give the highest priority to a Bill to remove the compulsion on LEAs to reorganise their schools on comprehensive lines'. Bill No 1, taken first of course, repealed Labour's 1976 Act. This went through Parliament with great rapidity (indeed it is notable how quickly Conservatives twice reversed Labour's actions on this issue). Comprehensive education once again was no longer 'National Policy'. The 1988 Act is clearly seen by its progenitors as signalling the death knell of the policy. But whether this Canute-like approach can be effective – in standing up against the tide of historical and social change – remains to be seen.

Social Paralysis and Social Change was the title of Smelser's book. He dealt with the nineteenth century; we are dealing with the twentieth – and indeed the very end of that. Yes, there has been change (and important gains have been won) but also paralysis. Shirley Williams's blocking of the single exam at sixteen in the late 1970s is a case in point. The massive power being built up within the system on this issue might have ensured radical, irreversible change – but the teeth of the movement were drawn in a welter of 'discussion' and the way thereby prepared for the hammer blows of the 1980s. At crucial moments there has been a clear lack of political will – in 1945-6, when a breakthrough might have been made; again in 1964-5 when decisive action required legislation; in the late 1960s when there was another chance, and finally in the mid-late 1970s when yet another opportunity was idly dissipated.

The deeper, historical question, it seems to me, is how to explain this lack of political will, of strength of purpose, which expressed itself on this particular issue – that of education. The Labour Party, in its time, produced and implemented tough policies in a number of areas – for instance, health, steel nationalization, even taxation. But in education the blows have been muted throughout the whole post-war period. To the detriment, I would suggest, not only of the working class but of other, middle sections of society and certainly, generally speaking, of the country as a whole. This is a matter for social (including educational) historians. It certainly requires explication – if only to make quite certain that, if and when another opportunity returns, as it certainly will, the same mistakes are not repeated, but, conversely are seized with both hands – agreed policies implemented with a sharp clarity of purpose and an unswerving determination.

Notes

[1] For this tradition, Joan Simon, 'Town Estates and Schools in the Sixteenth and Early Seventeenth Centuries', Chapter 1 of Brian Simon, ed., *Education in Leicestershire, 1540-1940* (Leicester, 1968).

[2] This evidence to the Spens Committee is summarised in Brian Simon, *The Politics of Educational Reform, 1920-1940* (London, 1974), pp258-9.

[3] The Labour Party's Education Advisory Committee held a total of 14 meetings between 7 February 1938 and 14 February 1940, the last meeting I attended. The minutes of these meetings are available in the Labour Party archives located at the National Museum of Labour History, 103 Princess Street, Manchester, M1 6DD. These archives do not appear to include the memoranda referred to in this article; these, and others, are at present in my possession. For later discussions in this committee on the multilateral school and related issues, Stephen Brooke, *Labour's War. The Labour Party during the Second World War* (Oxford, 1992), pp111-33.

[4] The discussion took place in *History Workshop Journal*. See H.D. Hughes, 'In Defence of Ellen Wilkinson'; *ibid.*, 7, Spring (1979), pp157-60; David Rubinstein, 'Ellen Wilkinson Reconsidered', *ibid.*, 7, pp161-9; and Caroline Benn, 'Comprehensive School Reform and the 1945 Labour Government', *ibid.*, 10, Autumn (1980), pp197-204. See also Betty D. Vernon, *Ellen Wilkinson* (1982).

[5] Michael Stewart, *Life and Labour* (1980), pp131-4; R.H.S. Crossman, *The*

Diaries of a Cabinet Minister, Vol 1., *Minister of Housing, 1964-66* (1975), pp132-3.
[6] I once met Fred (Lord) Mulley in the bar in the House of Lords and, having been introduced to him, told him I would be grateful for an interview sometime. He said he would be glad to accommodate me, but had held the job (Secretary of State) for so short a time as to make it scarcely worthwhile. Actually Mulley was Secretary of State for 15 months – not far below the average for the period 1940-1990 (21 months).

11. The Politicisation of Education: Implications for Teachers*

I

During the war there was a proliferation of new journals, cheaply printed, but made widely available. One, I believe, was called *New Writing*. It carried a series, by different hands, entitled 'The Way We Live Now'. The blackout, transport disruptions, rationing and shortages generally – all these created a totally new situation having many implications for ordinary humans. I suggest that the more or less total and rapid conversion to centralised control of education leading to arbitrary decisions, inept pronouncements, political in-fighting, the sudden emergence of obscure men onto the stage like a Punch and Judy show, resignations, crises – that all this creates, or is creating, a new situation, a new scenario. This might be reflected in a new series – 'The Way We Live Now'. Here is a contribution – it might be defined as a case study but I doubt if its research methodology would be considered worthy of an MA – call it a sketch entitled 'The Minister and the Trendies'.

But first a few words as background. Some may remember the battles that took place on streaming in primary schools in the 1960s. This was a crucial educational issue. At the start of that decade almost

---

* Lecture delivered to the Division of Education, University of Sheffield, May 1993.

all primary schools large enough were streamed – a product of the thinking and practice of the inter-war years reaching fruition at that time as Hadow reorganisation finally spread throughout the country.

Ten or fifteen years later, by the early 1970s, you could hardly find a single streamed primary school in the country. The change was dramatic. This was primarily a teacher movement – teachers held the power of decision. First the British Psychological Society in the late 1950s, then the Plowden Committee in the 1960s, recommended unstreaming. By the 1970s it was clear beyond all peradventure that the very process of streaming exacerbated differences between children present at the start of the junior or even the infant school. Streaming was shown to reflect class differences – it also discriminated against summer born children. Transfer between streams was shown to be minimal. Early stream placement, therefore, in most cases determined the child's entire future – especially with the 11+ lying ahead. Streaming also seemed to enhance behavioural problems in schools. A mass of research was carried through. By the mid-1970s there were no dissentient voices as I remember – nor even from any part of the political spectrum. This was one matter of high educational significance on which there was unanimity. It represented, in my personal view, one of the great achievements of a decade which was remarkable for its record of educational advance.

That's the background. But now, in the early 1990s, as is well known, Herculean efforts are being made to turn back the clock. This initiative is not coming from teachers, governors, parents, the hated 'educational establishment' or whatever. In keeping with the new scenario or 'The Way We Live Now', it is coming from on top – from ministers, secretaries of state, even, (probably) from the prime minister who was reported, just before the events I am about to describe, as having held a two day seminar on education (and related matters). It finds expression – and this is very much a 1990s phenomenon – in the tabloid press, alongside avid reporting of the misdemeanours of royalty and of (other) ministers. The technique is that of the 'inspired' news item – more usually (in our area) of a so-called 'report' by an 'educational correspondent' who has apparently been tipped off by some highly placed 'source' and who now proposes to reveal the truth to his or her (mostly his) gullible readers.

Here is the *Daily Mail* on 4 January 1993, a full fortnight *before* the release of *two* reports on primary education – one by the National Curriculum Council, the other by OFSTED.[1]

'Trendies Defeated'
by Ray Massey, Educational Correspondent

Below this a photo of John Patten looking stern. This is titled:

'Patten: Resolute'

Below the photo another headline in bold type:

'Minister orders schools to bring in streaming'

The story starts:

'Traditional teaching in which pupils are streamed according to their ability is to make a comeback in primary schools'.

It continues:

'Education Secretary, John Patten, is about to end three decades of 'progressive methods'. Advisers at standards watchdog OFSTED and the National Curriculum Council have told him that mixed ability teaching does not work'.

The article then asserts:

'Ministers want children to be grouped from their earliest years with others of roughly equal ability. They will insist that the most gifted receive sufficient stimulus'.

So much for the *Daily Mail*. But on the very same day (which indicates clearly some organising by someone somewhere), the *Daily Express* ran a similar story under a banner headline:

'Class streaming to put bright five year olds on fast track'

Here Gerald Greaves, 'education correspondent', reports:

'Primary school children will be streamed according to their ability under new education reforms. A review of the country's 20,000 primary schools will aim to stamp out trendy approaches in coping with children's different skills'.

These ideas, it is reported by both tabloids, are embodied in two reports due out in January. Both these news items, by the way, quote 'experts' and 'observers' (for example 'one observer said yesterday ...')

to enhance the impression of a top-level crack-down on the schools, to be powered by these two reports.

These asseverations about the imposition of streaming on primary schools by ministers were, by these two correspondents, beamed to millions – literally. But, in fact, when the NCC and OFSTED reports were published a full fortnight later (18 January) it was immediately clear that *neither* of these documents recommended a return to streaming.

The only mention either of streaming or of setting in the OFSTED report is the statement that, apart from the practice of ability grouping within a class, 'there is little evidence of any widespread move towards other forms of ability grouping such as 'streaming' or 'setting' (para. 44). The NCC report actually makes no mention of streaming whatever, but it does call for 'the setting of pupils according to ability where this is practicable' (para. 6.1). In line with much of the thinking of that council, its report does not find it necessary to provide one single reason and certainly no rationale to support the recommendation.

However that may be, it is surely clear that neither of these reports recommended a return to streaming, as the *Daily Mail* and *Daily Express*'s educational correspondents stated with such complete certainty and apparent authority. In fact neither of them got near to making such a recommendation. However this does not seem to have diverted the educational correspondents from their prey. When the two reports were finally released at a press conference in the embattled Sanctuary House (January 18th), the message handed to the press (presumably by ministers, Patten was present) seems to have been quite specific. Here is David Kerr of the *Sun*.

'Streaming is to be introduced into 22,000 primary schools to raise standards under a back-to-basics drive launched yesterday'.

This intention is ascribed specifically to John Patten who 'said the new moves were "plain, old-fashioned commonsense" '.

Now the *Daily Express* reappears saying that 'the package which allows for more pupils to be grouped by ability', is 'a further nail in the coffin for left-wing progressive education' (this rather nasty political shift or smear is adumbrated by education correspondent Gerard Greaves who also warns us that 'a Downing Street source' assured him that 'John Major took education very seriously' (so look out: big brother is watching you). On that day both the *Sun* and *Today* ran bullying leaders attacking teachers ('let's have more chalk and less talk', said the *Sun* – the relevance of that contribution to the question at issue is in doubt).

Would I be right in surmising that the message that is being got across by these means is the *ministerial* message – that what the tabloids are purveying is what the *minister* wants – what *his* views are. This seems to come out rather clearly in this case since the ministerial message, thus publicised, is *not* that of the two reports, which seem only to provide the occasion for the propagation of what appears to be the minister's view. I may seem at pains to labour this, but it is a crucial point in my argument.

Robin Alexander could tell us quite a lot about manipulation of the press, incidentally, so a few words also on his experience is appropriate – all grist to the mill in building up 'The Way We Live Now'. The way the Alexander report, as I prefer to call it (*Curriculum Organisation and Classroom Practice in Primary Schools*, 1992), was brought to the public typified the brutality of the conviction politics favoured by Kenneth Clarke, unregretted Secretary of State at that time. The report, which was produced in record time at Clarke's behest, was, in Robin Alexander's words, 'rushed out in type script at a press conference two weeks before schools and teachers could see it' (*Independent on Sunday*, 2.2.92). At this 'conference', educational correspondents were given fifteen minutes to read the report – at least 8,000 words in length, the argument being tightly compressed. 'Don't bother to read the document', Clarke told his assembled correspondents. 'You will find all the bullet points made in my press release'. (The use of the phrase 'bullet points' for a report on primary education seems symptomatic of the level, and character, of current ministerial thinking). This description comes from David Tytler, then educational correspondent of *The Times*, who shortly after resigned his job resenting, as in this case, the way education ministers abused the system of press briefing (see *Education*, 7.2.92).

Both the examples I have given – the treatment of the Alexander Report and of the NCC and OFSTED primary reports – are best seen as prime examples of the politicisation of education following the 1988 so-called 'Reform Act'. The grasp of power by the centre through this Act has had as one result – that ministers' actions in education must now be interpreted in terms of power struggles and other forms of internecine warfare actually *within* the governing (in this case the Tory) party. In the constant manoeuvring for position in a fluid political situation the Minister for Education must make his mark and, above all, enhance his reputation among the most important of the warring elements. Crises are, therefore, conjured up out of nowhere, providing opportunities for Napoleonic gestures in response. Collusion with the tabloid newspapers sets the scenario. So the Minister gains prestige (in both these cases with the right wing of his party), strengthening his claims for further advancement should opportunity arise. Indeed, apparently so successful has Kenneth Clarke been in this game that he was recently being seriously mooted as Major's probable successor. But it is education itself that suffers most directly from such priorities. And surely we can agree that this is no way to run the educational system of a highly complex, advanced industrial country such as Britain. That, then, is the first point I want to make and indeed to drive home with all the force I can summon. Apart from their inefficiency and indeed arbitrary nature, these procedures are discreditable to the country as a whole. They will certainly not encourage the raised standards that all claim they are in search of.

II

Having said that, let me switch the focus of discourse. The latest report on school performance of Britain's 16-19 year olds – that recently published by the National Institute of Economic and Social Research by Andy Green and Hilary Steedman, highlights just how far educational provision for British youth lags behind that provided for their contemporaries in France, Germany and especially Japan on a number of criteria.[2] The percentage of sixteen year olds reaching the equivalent of GCSE grades A–C in mathematics, the national language and one science (1990-91) is well over twice as high in Germany and France and nearly so in Japan as in Britain. The percentage obtaining a comparable upper secondary school qualification at eighteen or over (1990) is over twice as high in Germany and between two and three times as high in Japan where the figure reaches 80 per cent to our 29 per cent. The percentage of sixteen to nineteen year olds in full time or part time education and training in 1991 is 56 in Britain compared to nearly 88 in Germany and France and 94 in Japan. Sadly, we are getting used to figures (or comparisons) of this sort in Britain – indeed the gaps appear to be widening over time. But these are all sensitive criteria – or indicators, and they reflect a very serious historical neglect of educational provision for this age group – and indeed those of earlier age.

What do these three countries have in common compared to our own? There are no simple answers to this question and indeed we should beware of such. But in each of these countries (if we substitute Prussia for Germany before 1870), for a number of perhaps disparate reasons, the state intervened in education historically both earlier and more effectively than has been the case in Britain. This issue has been thoroughly analysed by Andy Green, in his *Education and State Formation: The Rise of Education Systems in England, France and the USA* (1990). As the author puts it in a recent article, 'The national education systems which developed in 19th century Europe did so in societies which were massively differentiated and fragmented'. This was the case in both France and Germany. National systems of education, Green continues, citing Durkheim, had as a primary function to foster social solidarity and national cohesion. Since that time, he continues, 'the state-forming role of educaton has increasingly involved meeting national economic needs as well as political imperatives'.[3] This central role of education in state formation is particularly striking in Japan, in the active and deliberate determination to modernise following the Meiji restoration in the early 1860s.

England, on the other hand, never had an equivalent experience. Perhaps partly because of our early development as a nation and of our equally early industrial development compared to other countries, education was never called upon to play the same role in state formation here as it was in France, Germany and Japan. Partly as a result, Green suggests, historically England 'has had one of the most pluralistic and "liberal" education system in the world'.[4] The general lack of state involvement left the field open to voluntary endeavour, and this on a wide scale not only in terms of the provision of education for the working class but also its provision for the various sections of the middle and upper classes through the re-structuring (by the state admittedly) of England's ancient endowed schools into some kind of system in the mid-late nineteenth century. I say 'some kind of' system since, compared to Prussian and French reorganisation in the nineteenth century we were far behind as Matthew Arnold consistently pointed out at the time. The result, Green argues, has been 'an immense plurality in types of school, curricula, examinations'; and it is by no means clear that the system which emerged, if it can be called a system, has empowered the majority of individuals more effectively than elsewhere. What is clear, however, is that the 'pluralism and diversity' that was brought into being has in fact 'been synonymous with the most hierarchical, elitist and class differentiated system in the world'.[5] This is now very much part of our problem.

'The current logic of international comparisons', Andy Green tells us, 'show that high achieving educational systems, like those in Germany, France and Japan, are generally those which place considerable emphasis on the public regulation and consistency of practice, whether this be in relation to the curriculum, assessment, teaching methods or learning materials. It is only governments in the grip of blind dogma', he goes on, 'who will ignore this and opt for the undiluted free market policies of countries like the USA, whose school standards are among the lowest in the OECD'.[6] The Japanese, incidentally, quite consciously rejected Nakasone's (then prime minister) 'liberalisation' policy – in full swing in terms of propaganda when I was there some years ago. They rejected it because it was seen as a threat to the state's traditional responsibility (since the Meiji restoration) for maintaining consistency of standards throughout the system – one which, incidentally, is deliberately organised with egalitarian objectives – especially since world war two. The same state responsibilities are accepted in both France and Germany. Here is a characteristic comment, made in 1989 just before unification, from Germany on British Thatcherite reforms of the 1980s:[7]

> To German observers the phenomenon of Thatcherite educational policy appears very strange. The tendencies towards privatisation and commercialisation of the educational system would encounter massive resistance in the Federal republic of Germany and would not be supported by a political majority ... most people believe that the school system has to be regulated by the state authorities in order to ensure effectiveness and social balance. For this we have the special term 'ordnungspolitik'.

In England and Wales it seems to me, our government is pursuing a contradictory policy – likely to lead to considerable confusion in the long run. Privatisation, commercialisation, creation of reliance on a market in schooling, league tables – these represent one prong of the attack. This new market orientation is bringing with it a whole new commercial culture – 'the culture of public relations, promotions, unit costing and quality control, where students are clients, parents are consumers, teachers are managers and learning is "value added" '.[8] It

181

can hardly be denied that this is a powerful trend having top-level approval and support. But recent legislation has also introduced another trend, symbolised in the secretary of state's four hundred odd new powers; powers of regulation, specifically and perhaps most importantly over the curriculum and assessment. So here is belated, if sharp and aggressive, intervention by the state into 'process' – what goes on in schools, teaching and learning, the National Curriculum and assessment. The sharply contradictory nature of these conflicting elements have been widely noted.

One outcome of the sudden arrogation of powers to the centre – scope for irresponsible behaviour by ministers – was highlighted in my case study on primary education. That sort of behaviour, together with the packing of curricular and assessment bodies with extreme right wing members of the governing party, can do no-one any good. But, I suggest, this does not imply that we should oppose an enhanced role for the state in controlling and evaluating educational development. I believe that the case for such a role has been made, and not only very recently – it has been evident over a long period. What has happened is that both the nature of the centralised powers suddenly acquired from 1988 and the way they have been exercised have been inept, ill thought out and inappropriate. Those in authority have been more concerned with winning immediate political advantage than with ensuring the long-term, ordered and healthy development of our educational system – or so it appears. Further the new pattern being brought into being is fundamentally flawed. You cannot effectively pursue two opposite objectives at the same time: God *and* Mammon. Or, if you do, you are likely to tear yourself into small pieces. And that is the danger now.

III

So ... what of the future? If I could simplify, we are faced with the alternatives of exercising serious, responsible, national and so central control over some key areas on the one hand, or of putting our faith in the blind operation of market forces on the other. Put like this, the conclusion is inescapable. We take the first alternative, and, as soon as the possibilities emerge, negate the entire move to determination by market forces.

What would be the implications of such a policy? There is time only to refer to the most important of these.

First, to ensure ordered, progressive development of our national system of education (or if you like, schooling), we will not set out, as priority, to destabilise, emasculate, and finally destroy local education authorities. Even today, in spite of all the blows directed at them, these still provide the essential infra-structure and support for local systems of primary and (mostly comprehensive) secondary education, and at the same time are locally and democratically accountable. In the last few years, as Stewart Ranson has shown very convincingly, a transformation has taken place in the direction of more user-friendly relations, enabling cooperative activities in place of the bureaucracy of the past.[9] But the attempt to create a market in education clearly implies their destruction, since a market requires free-standing, 'autonomous' schools (or autarkic units) all competing against each other. This is why current policy is antagonistic to the extent of including in the 1993 Education Act a section which, in effect, permits the actual abolition of local education committees, and why the so-called clause zero was lately introduced which, to all intents and purposes writes local education authorities out of the constitutional set up they have held since long before the 1944 Education Act was passed (clause zero became Sections 1 and 2 of the Act).

The whole of local government administration operates within statutory conditions laid down by parliament. Local authorities must comply with such legislation. There is a long experience of this relationship. If there are weaknesses, legislation can seek to correct these. Through this relationship, national standards, for instance as regards school buildings, are laid down for *national* observance. The same channels or techniques can be used to monitor and control other crucial aspects – for instance quality control relating to the curriculum and assessment. To destroy local education authorities, as the 1993 Education Act clearly sets out to do (particularly through the opting out sections), leaving them only with residual duties where they still exist is, I suggest, an act of educational vandalism of the first order, directed to enhancing the Mammon prong of the fork – the establishment of a market. We do not need to destroy our local authorities. On the contrary they need support and encouragement.

Another structural issue follows from this – and this is my second point. To create a market you need a diversity of products between which the customer exercises *choice*. Hence the title of the White Paper – 'Choice and Diversity'. Yet the national curriculum, in theory at least, ensures that all should be fed the *same* fare for most of the time.

183

Here the contradiction at the heart of recent legislation is most glaring. This is not, of course, preventing the government from pursuing its policy of diversity which relates closely to the destabilisation of LEA's. So instead of the single school for all from eleven to 16 – the locally maintained comprehensive school, which, incidentally, already contains very diverse elements, we now have city technology colleges, grant maintained schools, and now new types, the technology schools and even the new proposed technology colleges. To this witch's brew we must add church schools (which may proliferate), and private adventure schools of various kinds partially funded by the state through the assisted places scheme up to and including the prestigious or private public schools of yore. Probably no other country in the entire world has so 'diverse' a provision, nor one so riddled with class differentiation; that is part of the problem as I argued earlier.

It is not increasing diversification and differentiation that we need today, rather the opposite. Our school system needs *unification* – the focus needs to be on the development of main stream schooling up to sixteen and beyond. We do not need separate sectors, differentially funded in some quite arbitrary manner not open to public discussion. Now we have at least three 'sectors' in secondary education – that, I understand, is their official designation, each differentially funded: the grant maintained sector, the local authority sector, and the technical school (colleges) sector – not to speak of the city technology college sector. All these add to the complexity of the situation. It is the local authority sector, which contain the mass of the pupils, which suffers. The aim, I suggest should be to reduce this market element, as also the provision of 'diversity' in this sense. Is it any more than a cloak hiding enhanced differentiation?

IV

Perhaps we can turn now to the really important issues of teaching and learning. But for success these need a supportive context. The structural changes I have proposed are designed to ensure that.

The imposition of a national curriculum on all maintained schools in England and Wales has generally been accepted as a major break with the past in the sense of a direct intervention, by the state, in an area earlier held to be none of its business. It has, however, come to be widely accepted as defining what some have held to be an entitlement curriculum, enshrining in the law a broad general curriculum to be made available to all.[10] So far, whatever the criticisms, so good. Here is the other prong in the contradictory policy now being implemented – one which holds out a positive promise for the future.

But we can see very clearly at this moment, and in its recent history, that this initiative is also at risk, not so much from inept intervention by ministers (as indicated earlier) as from its subordination to the market policy which is determining the structural changes I have just discussed. And here the key issue is the league table policy. Suddenly we find that the whole national curriculum, *and* the assessment procedures linked with it, have as their *central purpose* the generation of league tables which, it is held, are essential to provide data allowing parents to make rational choices between schools. Whatever the perceived weaknesses of the tests, then, these must go ahead, and however much they offend the professionalism of teachers, yet they must be pushed through. Indeed as I write this argument has been taken one step further. Unless the Treasury has this data made available to it, John Patten has stated, how can they be expected to hand out money required for the educational enterprise as a whole?

We have often heard the argument that it is the civil servants who run the country, not the politicians – but it is not usually stated overtly by practising politicians actually in office. Perhaps we can see this as an argument in the last resort. So, through the league table initiative, the market economy and ideology penetrates centrally into the whole national curriculum and assessment initiative. That is not a healthy state of affairs and should be resisted – indeed, I would argue, nipped in the bud. There was certainly a warning in the notorious Red Book that preceded the 1988 Education Act that assessment would be used to enable comparisons between school and school but the whole four key stage assessment proposal was in fact sold to the teaching profession as centrally a *formative* assessment which would provide insights into individual pupils' development with a view to concerting means of overcoming difficulties and encouraging development generally. Of course this whole issue has been hotly argued over the years, Paul Black's TGAT (Task Group on Assessment and Testing) report has, to all intents and purposes, been jettisoned, as he has himself recorded in a striking address given in August 1992 to the Education Section of the British Association.[11] We are in an entirely new ball game as far as all that is concerned.

Perhaps I can conclude with a few random thoughts on this crucial issue – abstracting myself so far as possible from immediate concerns important though these are, because we do need to take a long term view.

The crucial issue, it seems to me, relates to the teacher's function of promoting learning on the part of the pupils or students. The development of the pupil's own abilities and skills, as well as his or her grasp of increasingly complex concepts and so his or her facility in higher mental functions – in this lies the whole complexity, skill and professionalism of the teacher, and this is as true of primary teachers as for secondary – perhaps more so. But this crucial role is obscured, perhaps deliberately, in the current jargon which defines the teacher as 'delivering' the curriculum – as if it were some kind of discrete entity, like a bag of fish and chips. From the delivery metaphor to its product, pencil and paper tests, is but a short step. And from these to league tables even shorter. I suggest that, in our long term thinking, we need to reject all these concepts and the practices that go with them.

Yes, let us have a national curriculum. Forty years ago, in the 1950's, the pioneers of comprehensive education were already thinking in terms of a common curriculum available equally to all and were beginning to define it. But let us now begin to rethink it, starting from the bottom up, based on first principles. We are loaded, it may be argued, with the original Red Book's subject based curriculum, and so we are. But that is no reason why we should not now begin to define, and elaborate, an alternative, this time based on educational principles. The world has moved on since 1904, and we need to keep pace. How this will be done I do not know – but we have plenty of brain power and committed people at our disposal. So I think we should go ahead. We certainly should not be satisfied with a 'slimming down' of the existing curriculum – as the secretary of state has instructed Sir Ron Dearing to do – and indeed the act of *instructing* the new authority what to do and how to operate is itself unacceptable.[12]

The same goes for assessment. The league table imperatives should be abandoned and consigned to the dustbin of history, as they deserve. Assessment must be a continuous process, and here teachers must play the central role. As a first step the Scottish system of banks of tests to be administered when thought appropriate by teachers might be acceptable. In general it is of crucial importance that assessment should follow the curriculum, not dominate it. Certainly there needs to be monitoring or quality control, as some call it, but this, as already suggested, could and should be a function of local education authorities, supported by a central authority. Indeed many were preparing to do just this when the Education Act of 1992 quite arbitrarily pulled the carpet from under their feet.

Of course there is a lot more one might say – about the need for flexibility in designing the curriculum, the need to provide scope for innovation and teacher based initiative generally, and above all the need for teacher involvement in decision making relating to teaching and assessment right across the board; and the need, to end where I began, to curb the powers of the secretary of state through effective devolution and control. Very careful thought needs to be put into constructing a viable and basically democratic process of consultation, research and experiment in definition of the curriculum, assessment and related matters. The unthinking rush to centralisation in the 1988 Act, in spite of severe warnings at the time, has already shown that the edifice erected is unviable, and even a threat to the ordered functioning of the system as a whole – indeed sometimes bringing it into ridicule. We cannot continue to allow instant decisions and immediate political advantage – even the whims of leading politicians – to govern developments in our field. All these devalue the process as a whole, leaving it vulnerable to yet further blows in the future. It is, I suggest, time for a change.

Notes

1 National Curriculum Council, *The National Curriculum at Key Stages 1 and 2* (January 1993); Office for Standards in Education (OFSTED), *Curriculum Organisation and Classroom Practice in Primary Schools, a follow-up report* (1993).
2 Andy Green and Hilary Steedman, *Educational Provision, Educational Attainment and the Needs of Industry: a Review for Germany, France, Japan, the USA and Britain* (NIESR, London, 1993).
3 Andy Green, 'Post-Modernism and State Education', *Journal of Educational Policy*, 1994, Vol. 9, No. 1, p81.
4 *Ibid.*, p80.
5 *Ibid.*
6 *Ibid.*, p79.
7 Detlef Glowka, 'Anglo-German Perception of Education', *Comparative Education*, 25(3), quoted in Green, *op.cit.*, p79.
8 Green, *op.cit.*, p77.
9 Stewart Ranson, *The Role of Local Government in Education* (London, 1992), especially chapter 7, 'The LEA and the Future'.
10 This was written before publication of the Dearing Report of January 1994, proposing abandonment of this objective for pupils aged 14 to 16.
11 Paul J. Black, 'The Shifting Scenery of the National Curriculum', in Clyde

Chitty and Brian Simon, eds., *Education Answers Back, Critical Responses to Government Policy* (London 1993).
[12] The proposals on the curriculum in the National Commission's report *Learning to Succeed* (1993), published since this lecture was given, provide a first class starting point for such a renewal; see especially Chapter 4, 'A Framework for Learning'.

Name Index

NAME INDEX

Subject Index

SUBJECT INDEX